THE SIBYL OF THE NORTH

THE TALE OF CHRISTINA QUEEN OF SWEDEN

CHRISTINA, QUEEN OF SWEDEN

THE SIBYL OF THE NORTH

The Tale of
CHRISTINA, QUEEN OF SWEDEN

BY
FAITH COMPTON MACKENZIE

With Illustrations

BOSTON AND NEW YORK
HOUGHTON MIFFLIN COMPANY
The Riverside Press Cambridge
1931

PLATES MADE IN GREAT BRITAIN
PRINTED IN THE U.S.A.

TO MY FRIEND
AXEL MUNTHE

CONTENTS

PART I

THE SIBYL OF THE NORTH

PART II

CAP AND BELLS

PART III

CARDINAL RED

LIST OF ILLUSTRATIONS

CHAPTER I

HEIR TO THE THRONE

" I WAS born covered with hair; my voice was strong and harsh," says Christina in her Memoirs, dedicated to God.

She came into the world masquerading as a male, and throughout her life she continued to do so as often as possible. She should have had a tall, straight body—a slim body to deck with doublet and hose and swashbuckling cape—a fine boy's neck to carry a sunburnt, clear-cut head crowned with a plumed cap. But her physical make-up was almost aggressively feminine. Her stature was small; she was plump, with a fine neck and bosom, and a perfect complexion. One shoulder was slightly higher than the other, a defect she took pains to conceal, though she says she could have cured it if she had taken the trouble. She dressed in fantastic parodies of man's attire—flat shoes with small black heels, a plain grey jacket, a black mariner's tie, a velvet cavalry cap which she put on and off like a man, ruffles at her wrist and her hair plainly braided. A concession to the feminine mode was a grey skirt, but this was short. So she appeared when Bulstrode Whitelock visited her on his embassy from Cromwell. She made no toilet except on state occasions, when she allowed her attendants to spend not more than half an hour upon it. She described herself as " the least curious in clothes of any woman ". Her hair was dressed once a week except on state occasions.

Her clothes were generally spotted with ink, and her indifference to appearances at a time when personal cleanliness was at best superficial, amounted to a measure of neglect which was sharply observed by her female critics. "Some people," she said once, "are silly enough to be slaves and martyrs to clothes and fashions and are unhappy if they do not spend their lives between the mirror and the comb. Tidiness is only for the idle."

Her hands were beautiful, masculine in form though very white, more indicative of her tendencies than any other feature; for her eyes, her magnificent eyes, might have belonged to either sex. They were full, lustrous eyes, glowing in an aquiline face.

Here is her portrait in regal robes. The little figure in the richly simple gown is posed like some portrait of Queen Victoria. One hand rests upon a book, her hair is plainly done, parted in the middle and adorned with a glittering ornament. A necklace of pearls, one brooch at her corsage, and two rings are all her jewels.

This soft, womanly exterior was the inadequate dwelling-place of a fiery genius with an insatiable lust for life and knowledge. If Christina had had a strong masculine body to match her mind she would have been one of the great figures of history. Most of her exalted schemes ended in smoke because her body got tired and reacted on her mind. Her pursuit of an idea was impassioned, but it simply wore her out; obstacles bored her, and in later life she met them at every turn. Besides, she had generally, as is the way with genius, squeezed all the juice out of a sensation before the average person would begin to realize that there was any juice in it. And then it was finished —cast away like an empty fruit-skin.

The story of her birth is like a fairy-tale. Her father, Il Rè d'Oro, the Golden King whose hair was the colour of honey and whose eyes sparkled like blue sea in sunlight —Gustavus Adolphus the Great—and his wife, Marie of Brandenburg, whom he adored, prayed for a son to be born. The stars were consulted and astrologers predicted the birth of an heir. Hopes therefore ran high in the Palace of Stockholm, when the Queen's labour was begun. So far she had only brought into the world two daughters, who had died as infants. But here was the longed-for heir about to be born; all the signs were in favour, and Gustavus Adolphus was as superstitious as any Papist.

It is not surprising that the sound of that strong, harsh voice and the sight of that hairy little body should fill the corridors with a rushing wind of silken skirts, and the Queen's ladies went tumbling over one another to be the first bearer of the good news. Haste and over-enthusiasm may have been responsible for the mistake. Yet the Queen herself was deceived; and, because the disappointment might have serious consequences, she was not undeceived until after the King. As soon as the truth was broken to her she took a violent dislike to the child, even to the extent, Christina says, of arranging accidents to put her out of the way.

The King had already ordered celebrations appropriate to the birth of a son and heir to the throne when his sister Catherine, Princess Palatine, brought the baby into his presence. The truth was made known to him. He took the odd little morsel into his arms, and in spite of the withering disappointment that must have been at his heart, he said: "Let us be grateful to God: I hope this daughter may be as a son to me."

He would not cancel or modify the public rejoicings. As a Prince she was welcomed by the people of Sweden, and as a Prince she was educated. From the moment that he took her in his arms she became her father's first care and dearest joy. Before she was two years old she delighted him when he took her to Kalmar, the great fortress, by applauding the salute of guns which the governor had hesitated to fire for fear of frightening her. She not only applauded, but made it clear that she wanted more. From that day she accompanied her father when he reviewed his troops. Mars, besides Venus and Mercury, was in the ascendant at her birth.

When she was four, on the 19th of May, 1630, her father presented her formally to the Estates as his heir. It was the eve of his departure for Germany on his last and greatest campaign for the Protestant cause. After his solemn speech of farewell was finished, Christina noticed that, though she had learnt a little " compliment " to repeat to the assembly, her father, occupied in conversation, had forgotten her. She pulled the tail of his coat and he, turning, took her in his arms. Moved, no doubt, by the fact that he had forgotten her for a moment, and that possibly he would be leaving her forever on the morrow, he wept as he embraced her before the assembly. Whether she repeated her little " compliment " or not after this she does not relate. But she cried for three days after his departure, so violently and so continuously that her eyes were seriously injured. This storm of emotion in so young a child, at a parting most children of that age would hardly realize, was regarded, and rightly, as of evil omen. She never saw Gustavus Adolphus again. But she wrote him two letters in German, and this is one of them.

> MOST GRACIOUS AND WELL-BELOVED FATHER,—After having assured Your Majesty of my humble filial respects, and prayed that the All-Powerful God grant you perfect health for the consolation of your obedient

daughter: I beg Your Majesty to come back very soon, and to bring me at the same time some pretty things. I am, thank God, in good health. I try to learn to pray every day.

I remain, Your Majesty's dutiful daughter,

CHRISTINA. P.S.

Gustavus Adolphus is one of the great figures of history. He fought among his soldiers as one of themselves, always in the forefront of the battle. He had the spirit of a Crusader, and with his high idealism went a genius for statecraft and the art of war. No wonder that English and Scottish volunteers flocked to fight under his banner. Such names as Ramsey, Ruthven, Stewart, Douglas and Hamilton were to be found among his officers. While at rest, after a battle, he would make music with his lute, singing softly to himself songs and hymns of his own composing.

The King was not unconscious of his consort's lack of character. He was devoted to her, with the passion great heroes often feel for women of feeble character, but he was too wise to be blind to her failings. Someone described her as "*Cette poupée encombrante et gênante*". Gustavus ensured that she should have no voice in the upbringing of Christina, by giving the child into the care of his sister Catherine and her husband, John Casimir, Prince Palatine, and by planning minutely the scheme of her education himself. Governors, preceptors and masters were chosen by him with meticulous foresight.

He appointed a Regency of five great officers of State to rule the kingdom during his absence at the wars. Foremost among these was the Chancellor Axel Oxenstierna, Gustavus's nearest friend and a man of genius little inferior to the King himself. Here was a great statesman, an incorruptible, devoted servant of the house of Vasa and of his country, with a profound knowledge of European affairs. " A tall, proper, straight old man . . . his hair grey, his beard broad and long, his countenance sober and fixed, and his carriage grave and civil." So Whitelock, the English ambassador, described him. Christina herself, much as she admired his qualities, thought him a little too slow and phlegmatic.

The other four members of the Regency were Baron Gabriel Oxenstierna, brother of the Chancellor; Baron Gyldenheim, a natural son of Charles IX, and half-brother of Gustavus Adolphus, who loved Christina, she says, as his own child; another Oxenstierna, cousin of the Chancellor; and Count Jacob de la Gardie, High Marshal, of French extraction, whose son Magnus played a sinister part in Christina's life.

Besides the Regency there were her tutors and governors. Axel Banér, brother of the Field-Marshal, was appointed her governor-in-chief. He was an accomplished courtier, a favourite of the King's and, Christina says, a companion of all his debaucheries. This calls for indignant comment by Arckenholtz, her chronicler, who declares that though Gustavus Adolphus loved amusement, he was never given to excesses, and was only known to have one child on the *côte gauche*, Count Gustaf Gustafsson de Wasaborg, to whom he behaved as a father should, directing his education with as much discretion as he did Christina's. This ingenuous remark of the single-minded Arckenholtz does not prove much, but the lofty strain in which Christina's own Memoirs are pitched may explain the use of the word " debauch " for an evening of august relaxation. However this may be, Gustavus Adolphus was so devoted to Banér that he made him a gentleman of the bedchamber, shared his bed with him before he was married

—and afterwards, when the Queen was absent. Christina found him an excellent courtier, but deplorably ignorant, knowing no language but his own (almost a criminal offence in her eyes), much given to wine and women, but withal an honest man.

Gustavus Horn, her *sous gouverneur*, was more to her liking. He was a distinguished general, had travelled, and spoke passably several languages. Though he suffered from the vices of the age, he had at least a veneer of cosmopolitan address. But her favourite was John Matthaie, who was her instructor in religion, letters and the sciences. She says of him that he was suspected of a strong leaning towards Calvinism. " I do not know if he was misjudged, but at least it was the only fault that could be found with him. At any rate, it did not matter at all whether he was Calvinist or Lutheran. I was not going to be either."

This good man became Bishop of Strengnas, but, by reason of his broad-minded tolerance and desire for general reconciliation of religion, the jealous and bigoted ecclesiastics in power after Christina had abandoned her throne obliged him to resign his bishopric. Christina, however, never forgot him and helped him liberally till his death. Gustavus Adolphus, who fought and died for his religious convictions (with an eye always upon the Baltic) had no suspicions of Matthaie's alleged Calvinistic leanings or he would not have entrusted his child's religious education to him. He naturally dreaded more than anything the possibility of her being perverted from Lutheranism to Calvinism. The prospect of so dreadful a retrogression as later occurred was mercifully hidden from him.

Gustavus Adolphus was killed in the battle of Lützen on November 6, 1632, in the fourteenth year of the Thirty Years' War. Wallenstein had consulted the astrologers, and finding that the stars were hostile to Gustavus, he decided to give battle. There was a dense fog through which Gustavus rode at lightning speed at the head of his cavalry. His arm was shattered by a musket-ball, and as he was being led away by an attendant he was shot in the back. There are many theories as to the hand which dealt this death-blow. Arckenholtz is convinced it was the hand of a traitor. Partly because of the fog, and partly because of his great speed, there were few witnesses of his death. The Duc de Saxe Lauenbourg was with him, and is one of those inculpated. A curious story came from Saxony fifty-three years afterwards. An old man confessed that he had been with Gustavus when he was wounded, that he had shot him with his pistol and stolen the spectacles that Gustavus always used for short sight. When he confessed, he delivered up the spectacles to his confessor, from whom they were bought by a Swedish gentleman, M. André Groedging, and deposited in the Swedish archives. This tale is legendary, but is less revolting than the notion of a trusted officer being the murderer.

The appearance of the King's charger, galloping with blood-stained saddle through their ranks, announced to the Swedes that their beloved leader was dead. When the battle was over and search was made for his body it was found buried beneath a heap of dead, stripped, robbed, and covered with blood, trampled almost out of all recognition by horses' hoofs.

Christina was six when her father died, and, though her grief at the time was passionate, when, two years later, his body was brought in state to Sweden, the remembrance of him had faded, and as she remarks herself, " children who expect to inherit a throne are easily consoled for the loss of a father ". Besides, two years is as long as eternity to a child of eight. Not only were the tedious ceremonies in which she had to take part exceedingly irksome, but a new development in her relations with her foolish mother threatened to cast a blight over the rest of her childhood.

After persistently neglecting the child whose sex she so deeply resented, Marie Eleanore suddenly assumed, after the death of her husband, an exaggerated maternal attitude which demanded the continuous presence of Christina at her side. This would have been tiresome under any circumstances, but the extravagant mourning which became simply an unpleasant form of self-indulgence and the excessive affection lavished upon herself were more than Christina could bear. She writhed under her mother's caresses. Her early childhood had been spent in the company of men—big men, too, the pick of Sweden. The Princess Palatine, the only woman with whom she had been on intimate terms, was strong-minded, not given to vapours and sentimentality. Marie Eleanore's display of feminine weakness was something new and revolting. Christina could not endure this kind of thing, and as she grew older she had less and less toleration for women. She once said she liked men not so much because they were men as because they were not women. Marie Eleanore was no doubt partly responsible for her daughter's impatience with the average of her sex. Christina had very much the point of view of the homosexual male in regard to women. There were certain ladies distinguished for their beauty or wit whom she admired almost beyond the bounds of what is compatible with admiration. The average female—*la donna che pensa con l'utero*—bored and disgusted her, but she readily admitted her usefulness, and the ladies-in-waiting she dragged about Europe with her were poor, homely creatures whom she treated with the generosity of a slave-owner.

She even denies woman the capacity of governing a kingdom, and does not exempt herself from the indictment, though she does not mention Queen Elizabeth. All women, she says, who have reigned, or pretended to reign, have made themselves ridiculous in one way or another. At sixty-three, looking back at her ten years' reign over Sweden, what particularly was in her mind when she wrote that paragraph in the biography which, though it extended no farther than her eighth year, showed signs of being nothing more than a justification of herself before a censorious world? If she had not been intimidated by the clamour of the pornographists what a biography she could have written—if their calumnies had not driven her to the other extreme in self-defence! It would have ranked with Casanova or Benvenuto, if she could have written as she talked, and told her tale freely with her keen and fiery wit.

. . . .

Marie Eleanore imprisoned herself and her daughter in candle-lit rooms hung with black. In these rooms hideous dwarfs and buffoons crept and capered; the heart of Gustavus Adolphus reposed in a coffer in the very room where Christina lay through long, uneasy nights beside her mother. The velvety walls were full of dark shadows. It was not surprising that Christina welcomed the hours of her lessons, when she could take refuge in her tower and bury herself in study, spurred on by the tutors who helped her to forget that dismal room below where dwarfs bobbed and wambled, tapers flared, and a mournful woman in sable draperies hung about her neck and bathed her resisting head with tears.

This could not go on, and it was obvious that

Christina's nerves were affected by such an unnatural existence. Though Gustavus Adolphus had expressly ordered that she should not be under her mother's influence, it was hardly possible, immediately after his death, to deny his widow access to the child, who, she now declared, was all that was left to her in life. Once the child was yielded, to release her was difficult. Any attempt at a change brought on a storm of tears and entreaties from the Queen-Mother which it was hard to resist, especially as the Grand Chancellor was still in Germany and his authority lacking.

So for two years Christina shared her mother's life, endured her caresses, her moods and her persistent mourning, until Axel Oxenstierna returned from Germany, and Marie Eleanore herself provided an excellent loop-hole by criticizing the education of her daughter. Here was an opportunity which the Regents were not slow in taking. They could not, they said, allow any interference with the education of the Queen. The minute instructions left by her father were sacred, and were being carried out faithfully. (All, it must be admitted, but the clause relating to the Queen-Mother.) Christina was restored to the guardianship of her uncle, Prince Palatine, and his wife, and Marie Eleanore retired in a rage to her castle at Gripsholm, in Sudermania. Christina was glad to be back among her cousins. Her favourite was Charles Gustavus who, she decided, should eventually be her husband.

And now the education began in good earnest. Matthaie found his religious instruction no easy matter. Christina, from babyhood, accepted nothing without question; she was born a sceptic, and such problems as the following must have presented themselves often to the devoted teacher. In her eighth year she was taken to hear the annual sermon on the Day of Judgment. Horrified, she demanded of Matthaie why she had not been warned of this. Would it happen to-night, and what would become of her? Matthaie soothed her with some conventional hope that if she were good she would go to Paradise. The second year she was sarcastic about it, and the third year she laughed and asked if all the rest of religion was as much of a fable as this Day of Judgment which never came. Her teacher rebuked her sternly for this, and even threatened her with the whip, at which, she says, she quelled him with a glance; but that day, whatever belief she may have had in her father's religion died. She says she invented one of her own, and though for form's sake she attended the dreary Lutheran church, her example was not of much use to her subjects, for she played with her dogs or read books throughout the interminable sermons.

If she was difficult on the religious question, she made amends to her tutor in her enthusiasm for the Classics. She soon mastered enough Greek and Latin to enjoy reading them in the original, and by the time she was fourteen she was enjoying Cicero, Livy, Tacitus and the rest, as well as speaking and writing French, German, Italian, Spanish and, of course, Latin and Greek. Science, which was also Matthaie's province, she regarded as a recreation rather than a study, and she showed as early as this the passion for rare books and manuscripts that ultimately made her library one of the most famous in Europe. She studied twelve hours a day when possible, because she liked it. There was no forcing by her tutors—it was not necessary. "I had an insatiable desire to know everything," she says. "*Tout savoir!*"

In spite of this bookishness she was not a prig. If Minerva occupied one side of the medal, on the other was Diana. She was one of the finest riders in Sweden. There was no horse she could not master. Hours were spent in the saddle in man's habit—sometimes ten at a stretch. She would throw herself on the bare ground for rest, regardless of heat or cold or lack of food, drinking nothing but spring water. Wine or beer were odious to her, and she was once chastised for stealing the dew water intended for her mother's toilet, because she was given nothing but wine to drink when under her care. Chanut says in his Memoirs that she only slept five hours, and Christina alters this in the margin to "three hours". No one could persuade her to spare herself, and when her ladies- (and gentlemen-) in-waiting began to yawn she would send them all to bed. She slept little, not because she needed little sleep, but because all her hours were precious. So many were occupied with State business that there was not time for her books, her horses, her dogs, her hunting.

The eye of all Sweden, and soon of all Europe, was upon her, and she was duly conscious of it, and enjoyed it obviously. Conceited, vain, arrogant, egotistic—all these she was, but she never had a smug moment.

Equally important and as much enjoyed as her studies with Matthaie were the hours spent daily with the Grand Chancellor Axel Oxenstierna, when he instructed her in her duties as ruler of her people, in statecraft and the conduct of war. She astounded him by her precocious insight. She discussed the most complicated problems of the war situation with a breadth of vision and understanding seldom found in a woman, much less in a child of ten. She had never known anything but a state of war, and while she was sitting at the feet of her great preceptor, her country, whose main army had been almost annihilated at Nördlingen in 1634, was re-establishing itself as an invincible Great Power, partly by the genius of Oxenstierna himself, who bought off Poland with a twenty-six years' truce, arranged a large subsidy from France, and appointed John Banér Commander-in-Chief. The victory of Wittstock followed, and under Banér the army regained what it had lost since the death of Gustavus Adolphus. In 1640 the health of the leader began to fail. Christina wrote to her uncle:

> Banér is dangerously ill and in all human probability will not recover. Nobody troubles about this here. They think they can find someone to take his place, but men such as he are not shaken out of one's sleeve. Things will go ill if Banér dies. . . .

She was partially right. When Banér died, in 1641, the Swedish army went to pieces again, much as it did at the death of Gustavus Adolphus. Mutiny and corruption spread like a plague. But Sweden's stock of great leaders was not yet exhausted. Lennart Torstensson, " the equal of Banér in genius, his superior in energy, mastering by the greatness of his soul a body wasted by captivity and disease ", was called from his retirement to save Sweden and her army. This brilliant soldier, who was known as Blixten, from his swift and incalculable movements in action, had been page to Gustavus Adolphus in early days, and at twenty-seven was in command of the Swedish artillery in the battle of Breitenfeld, when the King himself had commanded the right wing. A whole day's battle it had been, and had marked the turning-point of the Thirty Years' War, and had raised Sweden to the rank of a Great Power. In a later action Torstensson was taken prisoner for nearly a year, which helped to shatter his health. But he was back doing great things with Banér until 1641, when he was compelled to retire from ill-health—he was a martyr to gout—and was made a Senator, and no doubt expected to end his days peacefully in the Riksdag. But scarcely two months had passed when Banér died, and Torstensson was recalled to be Generalissimo of the armies. His arrival with fresh forces and money put life into the army, and the period of his command was a series of brilliant engagements (during most of which he was carried about in a litter) culminating in the decisive victory of Leipzig, in 1642. No sooner was the situation improving in Germany than trouble with Denmark, which had long been threatening, was brought to a head indirectly by no less a person than Marie Eleanore, the Queen-Mother, who had been sulking and plotting in her castle at Gripsholm since she had been deprived of all power over Christina.

It is not really surprising that she sulked. From her point of view it was monstrous that she should be ignored so completely by the guardians of the young Queen. After all, she was her mother, and she had been the adored wife of Sweden's greatest ruler and a figure of some importance. The situation was humiliating indeed. She had never loved Sweden; now she hated it, and certainly hit upon an effective revenge. There was one person who appreciated her situation, and that was the elderly but still vital King Christian IV of Denmark. Her flight from Gripsholm was melodramatic and absurd. She spent several days in elaborate preparation for it, and then shut herself up with one lady-in-waiting in a room opening on to the castle grounds, on the pretext that she wished to meditate and fast. At dead of night she and her companion crept to where a carriage was awaiting them, posted to Nyköping, where a sloop took them on board a Danish man-of-war sent by Christian, who was fondly awaiting her on the island of Gottland. At least gossip said it was fondly. Whatever the motive for this " tender pilgrimage ", it might as well have been made quite openly, as no one in Sweden had the least objection to her departure on whatsoever pretext. But the fact that she had been aided secretly in her flight by Denmark was just what was necessary to unloose the flood of hatred and jealousy which had so long been on the point of overflowing. The story of this jealousy is too long to tell here; it goes back to Knut, and Harald Blue Tooth, and a contributary cause had always been the control of the Baltic.

Oxenstierna sent secret instructions to Torstensson who was in Moravia, and rushed his armies in an incredibly short time across Prussia and the Danish frontier. In a lightning flash Jutland was occupied by the Swedish army. King Christian straightway set about himself the equipping of his navy, and in June, 1644, met the Swedish fleet that was to take Torstensson to the islands, and the great sea battle of Kolberger Heide, which lasted ten hours, was fought, with the heroic old King standing on the quarter-deck throughout it, though an exploding gun wounded him in thirteen places and he lost an eye. This battle of Jutland was as indecisive as a later famous one. Both sides claimed the victory. A few months afterwards, another tremendous fight gave the victory to Sweden, and Denmark was obliged to give in. Oxenstierna was for pressing hard terms, but here Christina's individual judgment is clearly shown. She could not but be moved by the tragedy of the fine old King who, in spite of his sixty-eight years, braved the fury of desperate engagements only to be vanquished. She was inclined to be a generous victor. And not for sentimental motives only. Her political foresight prompted her to make a peace reasonable enough not to be broken. No one was to be trusted in those days when war hung like a miasma over Europe. And in any further trouble who would not be glad to side against Sweden with her dangerous Baltic supremacy? Oxenstierna was obliged to recognize the justice of Christina's point of view, and when he returned from the peace conference at which France had been a mediator, Christina made him a Count, a high dignity in Sweden, endowed him with a large estate, and made a remarkable speech in his praise in the Senate.

CHAPTER II

"CHRISTINA, BY THE GRACE OF GOD——"

BEFORE peace with Denmark was established, Christina came of age on her eighteenth birthday, December 8, 1644. This was a magnificent occasion. She sat on a silver throne, surrounded by her counsellors of state, and took the oath as *King* of Sweden, promising among other things to maintain the national religion.

Now she took command; the Regency had done its work. It was exciting to be King of a great military nation, and it would be amusing to snub Oxenstierna occasionally. Though the Chancellor had been her guide from childhood, she had long ago decided upon her policy when she came of age. Oxenstierna, though he was constantly in treaty with Richelieu and recognized the importance of France as an ally, was deeply distrustful of that country. Christina, on the other hand, was fascinated by the idea of that great nation of civilized and cultured human beings. A fine military history was all very well, but as far as intellectual things went, Sweden was in outer darkness. Brilliant statesmen and soldiers—plenty of them—but with the exception of dear old Matthaie, there were few people of her own nation about her who really cared a fig for philosophy or the fine arts.

Pierre Chanut, the French Resident, had done much to draw her to his own country. Not only was he the best type of French gentleman, " an ambassador of the first class ", and a man of high honour and ability, but he was one of the most learned scholars of his time, and naturally Christina rejoiced in his company. He had travelled, knew many languages, alive and dead, and was, best of all, an intimate friend of the philosopher Descartes. Christina had studied Platonism from an early age, and, as we shall see, was avid in her search for new philosophies. If there was anything new, she must know it. *Tout savoir!*

There was, however, one subject on which Christina was content to be, if not ignorant, at any rate ill-informed, and that was home politics. She was aware that there was a certain amount of disaffection and unrest among her people, but her advisers had not over-emphasized its importance nor the urgency of reform in these matters. The aristocrats ruled, and the cry of the people, worn out by continual war, heavy taxation, and the tyranny of the nobles, was as far as possible kept from her ears. As she was zealous in her attendance at the Senate, she could not have failed to hear this subject discussed. In the Senate no question could be debated that was not first introduced by the Sovereign, and she did attempt, sometimes successfully, to redress a few of the glaring wrongs from which her humble subjects were suffering. But home politics bored her. Already her mind was stretching out to other lands than Sweden, though for the moment it went no further than the desire to attract to her Court the distinguished figures of literature and art. It was obvious that this could not be done on any scale until the war was over; therefore the war must be ended as soon as possible. Christina concentrated upon this object with all her energy. Negotiations for peace had begun in 1641, but the real congress did not meet until 1645, and to it went the Chancellor's son, John Oxenstierna, and Adler

Salvius as Sweden's plenipotentiaries, and this was the cause of Christina's first real difference with Axel Oxenstierna.

As usual the military party did not really want peace, and even the Chancellor was not enthusiastic about it. He advised his son to hold up negotiations as long as possible, and to be adamant over Sweden's terms. Christina, however, took Adler Salvius into her confidence and exhorted him to do all in his power to hasten the end. The two plenipotentiaries were already on the worst of terms, Salvius the man of modest birth, risen to high estate by sheer merit, being treated with haughty contempt by John Oxenstierna, whose only claim to his position was that he belonged to one of the first families. The clash of contending interests and personalities at Osnabrück, where the Protestant peacemakers were meeting, could not but resound in Stockholm, and resulted in high words between the Queen and her Minister in full Senate.

The Peace of Westphalia, which wound up the Thirty Years' War at last, was finally concluded in October, 1648, but peace between Christina and her Chancellor was further off than ever. In fact, so strained were their relations that the Chancellor wished to retire from Sweden; a suggestion gladly welcomed by the Queen, but leading to such a storm of protest in the Senate that she was obliged to ask him to stay, and patched up a half-hearted truce with him. The fame of Oxenstierna throughout Europe was a thorn in Christina's side. Whatever good things were done in Sweden were put to his credit, though Christina was conscious of being responsible for many wise measures, and she prided herself specially upon her influence over the proceedings of the Peace conference. Her delight knew no bounds when the courier arrived announcing that the pact was signed. A gold chain worth six hundred ducats was presented to him, public rejoicings were ordered, cannon fired, Te Deums sung, and at last the sums which had been poured out on war all these years could be diverted with a clear conscience into other channels. But not much was left. The Swedish coffers had been depleted for many years before Christina came to the throne; the Regency had been wildly extravagant, ministers and officials filling their own pockets on a grand scale; Crown lands were bought up by the nobles, and the peasants suffered accordingly by the tyranny of their new landlords. This sale of Crown lands had begun in Gustavus Adolphus's time, and was one of the chief causes of the people's discontent. The nobles were omnipotent; they alone benefited by the war, they alone were untaxed and absolutely free to oppress and grind the peasants at their will. Christina faced this problem half-heartedly. It was indeed a difficult one to solve.

Another exceedingly tiresome problem had been occupying Christina in the meanwhile, and that was the problem of avoiding marriage. For three years Prince Charles Gustavus, her cousin and son of the Prince Palatine, had been pressing her to marry him. As children they had played at being engaged, and even in 1644 she must have imagined she was in love with him, for she wrote:

> My love is so strong that it can only be overcome by death, and if, which God forbid, you should die before me, my heart shall be dead for anyone else, but its memory and affection shall follow you to eternity. Perhaps you will be advised to ask for my hand now and openly, but I implore you by all that is sacred to have patience for yet a year, till you have had more experience in war, and I have got the crown on my head. [The coronation was yet to come.]

Remember the old saying, "He waits not too long who waits for something good."

This tone was encouraging to the ardent suitor, who forthwith went to the war and was nearly blown to bits getting the necessary experience; but when he came back full of honours to claim her hand he found it cold and unresponsive. She did not exactly say "No", but she implied that he would still have to wait for that "something good".

To tell the truth, Christina's affections had not been too firmly fixed upon Charles Gustavus. There was one person whom she loved to "caress", and that was Count Magnus de la Gardie. He was the son of the High Marshal and of beautiful Ebba Brahe, the only other woman besides his Queen whom Gustavus Adolphus had ever loved. De la Gardie had French blood, and compared to the excellent but perhaps somewhat rough-and-ready Swedish courtiers that surrounded her, he shone as brightly as a diamond in a heap of pebbles. On this handsome young courtier the Golden King's daughter showered such conspicuous public favours that the world naturally supposed he was her lover. As history does not tell what private favours he enjoyed, it is useless to speculate on their relations. At any rate, had he been her lover, she could not have honoured him before the world more extravagantly than she did. Rank and office were bestowed, vast estates bringing in incredible sums, and most marked of all her public favours was the embassy on which she sent him to the French Court. By this time he was married to Christina's cousin, one of the Prince Palatine's daughters, sister of Charles Gustavus.

Outside any partiality the Queen may have had for his person, there is no doubt that de la Gardie was the ideal figure for the mission to France. No expense was so much as considered in the equipment of this embassy. It was done in magnificent style, and even the French were impressed. Chanut sent a private warning that the more this young ambassador was caressed, the better pleased Queen Christina would be.

France took the hint, and fêted the brilliant young man and his suite with a succession of balls, plays and amusements of all kinds. The object of his embassy, the strengthening of friendship between the two nations, was not forgotten in the whirl of entertainments. Madame de Motteville says, "He spoke of his Queen in terms so passionate and respectful that it was easy to suspect in him a feeling more tender than that which he owed her as a subject." His visit was a success from every point of view. There was some trouble in Sweden about an enormous sum which he had borrowed in Paris. The war was not yet over when this embassy sailed for France, and there was horror in the Senate when the news arrived that de la Gardie had borrowed what might have been enough money to help the Swedish army to victory. In vain Christina took the blame upon herself. She had authorized this extravagance, she said. The Chancellor, who had discouraged de la Gardie's embassy from the first and was only too pleased to find some just cause of complaint, was obstinately resolved in his disapproval. So uncomfortable did he make it for the Queen that she was driven to beg her friend Salvius to lend her privately the same sum, which should be devoted to the needs of the army.

De la Gardie returned after a year in Paris, and was amply rewarded for the success of his embassy. He seems to have kept his position as first favourite at Court. The only other person who held Christina's heart in those days was Ebba Sparre, her maid-of honour. This lovely, delicate creature was truly beloved of the Queen. She was one of those ladies (already noted) distinguished for their wit and beauty whom Christina deigned to admire almost beyond the bounds of what is compatible with admiration. . . .

Someone said of Christina that she had been taught everything " except to love ". It is true that her childhood was perhaps peculiarly barren of the sweeter sensibilities. She had no mother's knee at which she could prattle and learn the mysteries of nursery lore. But even if she had had a worthy mother, would she have spent more time than she could possibly help at the maternal knee? Would she not have fiercely questioned and scarcely tolerated the nursery legends, as she questioned and disdained the religious teachings of Matthaie? Her spirit sprang like a lupin-seed in the hot sun, clear and direct —with a clean rush through the air to its own individual self-found bourne. There it grew, detached as the spirit of genius must be—lonely, egocentric, wistful sometimes —deprived by its very nature of ordinary emotional commerce.

. . . .

Charles Gustavus was becoming impatient. Other suitors were attracted to the blue-eyed, flaxen-haired little Queen whose gifts were creating such a stir in Europe, and whose throne would be such a pleasant one to share. Two Danish Princes, the young Elector of Brandenburg, Philip of Spain, the King of Hungary, everyone, in fact, of any importance, and a few that were of none. There was no time to be lost.

At last Christina consented to an interview with Charles Gustavus at which Matthaie and Magnus de la Gardie were to be witnesses. The presence of the latter was a delicate cruelty which must have added zest to the conversation.

The rather heavy, boorish young man was confronted by his brother-in-law, the debonair favourite, obviously in full power, and no doubt enjoying the situation excessively.

"I must tell you," said Christina, "that I cannot promise to marry you at all. I can only promise that I will not marry anyone else."

This was not much good to Charles Gustavus. It brought him no nearer to the throne. But then she dropped her startling bomb, composed of how many elements, half-formed desires, dreams, and probably a lightning flash of inspiration. To avoid matrimony, to evade the horror of providing with her own body an heir to the throne! She knew it was this necessity that was urging the States to demand her marriage, not any regard for her happiness. And nearly everyone had his own axe to grind. Even Oxenstierna had dared to contemplate the idea of his own son Eric as consort. There was much talk about it, but there is no evidence that Christina did more than laugh at the notion.

"I will promise you something else," she said to Charles. "Supposing I decide never to marry, I will make you my successor to the throne. You shall be my heir."

However much this announcement may have startled and thrilled Charles Gustavus, he protested that unless he could look forward to marriage with her he had no further interest in life, and would leave Sweden never to return. Christina was not in the least taken in by this high, romantic tone, and when he reproached her with her childish promises, she assured him that he should be very grateful for ever having been considered, even in her childish days, worthy of so great an honour.

Here, no doubt with a glance at the sleek favourite,

Charles made a disparaging remark about other aspirants for her hand and favours, citing especially Eric Oxenstierna and persistent rumours. Christina indignantly declared at this that if Charles listened to such ridiculous gossip, he was not worthy of her great project for him. Charles played the forlorn lover to the end of this interview.

"At least I may write?"

"To your father and Matthaie. Yes."

With this he had to be content, and he left her and her two advisers, giving no outward sign, at any rate, of elation at the prospect of some day occupying the throne of Sweden not merely as consort but as King. Besides, probably he felt that this fantastic promise was unlikely to materialize.

Christina went out on to the terrace of the Palace and watched him ride away—watched him till he was out of sight.

Was there a tinge of regret for the love of her childhood as she shaded her brilliant eyes with that finely shaped boy's hand of hers? Or was it perhaps that Magnus was standing behind her, and it was good for him to be tantalized a little bit, after that rather too triumphant interview? Probably something of both.

There are many theories about Christina's aversion from marriage. She herself is responsible for several. As a child she said, when told of the Catholic idea of celibacy as the highest state of moral perfection: "Ah, how fine that is. That shall be my religion."

In her Memoirs comes the following remarkable passage:

> My ardent and impetuous temperament has given me an inclination for love no less than ambition; into what misfortune might not so terrible an inclination

have led me, if Thy grace had not made use even of my defects to correct me of it! My ambition, my pride, incapable of submitting to anyone, my disdain, despising everyone, marvellously preserved me; and by Thy grace, Thou hast added thereto so fine a delicacy that Thou hast preserved me from an inclination so perilous for Thy glory and my happiness; however near the precipice I have been, Thy hand has held me back. Thou knowest, whatever evil tongues may say, that I am innocent of all the wrong-doing with which they have tried to blacken my life. I vow that if I had not been born a girl, the inclinations of my temperament would probably have led me into terrible licence. But Thou who has made me love glory and honour more than any pleasure all my life, Thou hast preserved me from the ills into which the opportunities, the freedom of my condition, and the ardour of my temperament might have precipitated me. I should no doubt have married, had I not been conscious of the strength Thou hast given me to forswear the pleasures of love. I knew the world too well to be ignorant that a girl who wishes to enjoy life must have a husband; above all, a girl of my rank, who marries but to gain a subject, or rather a slave to her will and caprice. . . . Had I been conscious of any weakness, I should have known how, like so many others, to marry for pleasure's sake, and enjoy my good fortune; and I should not have had that invincible aversion from marriage (of which I have given so many striking indications) had it been necessary to me. But Thou hast given me a heart which could devote itself only to Thee; Thou hast formed it of such an admirable and vast capacity only to be filled by Thee. . . . This heart was Thine from the moment it first beat in my breast. . . .

This, it must be remembered, was written in middle age. She expressed herself in simpler language, but to much the same effect, at the time.

" I would rather die than be married. I could never allow anyone to treat me as a peasant does his field."

When pressed by her councillors to choose a husband, she said:

" I am as likely to give birth to a Nero as an Alexander. I would rather designate a good Prince and successor capable of holding the reins of government than marry at this moment."

That idea was not at all acceptable to her government. If Christina was not going to marry and produce an heir, they saw no reason why she should dictate her successor. The House of Vasa would die out, and the succession might go into—almost any quarter. Christina was well aware that if she did not produce an heir in one way or another, the Estates might elect whom they chose as her successor—an Oxenstierna, a Brahe—and she had enough feeling for the House of Vasa to want to perpetuate as far as possible that great family in Swedish history. Charles Gustavus was at least the nephew of Gustavus Adolphus, and she was determined that he should succeed her, whatever the Estates might say. They said a great deal, on February 23, 1649, when she presided at a Senate to discuss the succession. The question of her marriage was also involved, and the severest of her critics was her old tutor Matthaie, who said:

" Your Majesty is obliged to marry, by the Decrees of the Realm."

" No one on earth can persuade me to that unless I settle it myself. I don't deny that I may do it one day. To marry for the good of the Realm, that's a great motive! But when I find a means as good to secure the Realm, what more can be asked of me? The Act of Succession does not prevent me from marrying. What I promised to Charles Gustavus I shall religiously observe. But you shall not know now what it was that I promised him. I might marry him after he has been declared Successor to the Throne, a declaration which could be made now with advantage, but no one in heaven or earth can constrain me to it."

"For Your Majesty there is no risk. But for us there is great danger if we disregard the Decrees of the Realm."

"No one in the world can make me change the plan I have made. If I marry I shall marry no one but Charles Gustavus. But I will not tell you now if I shall marry; you will know at my coronation."

When reminded that all the world would talk when it heard of her decision, she said, "When they've talked enough they'll soon find something else to amuse them", and indeed she herself was to provide them with a series of sensations for the rest of her life.

Though the whole Senate was against her, she won her point in the end, and the Act of Succession was signed, though the Chancellor remarked as he signed it that, if he had the choice, he would prefer to enter his grave rather than lend himself to such a document. Charles Gustavus ceased to urge marriage, but retired tactfully to his estates on the island of Öland, and refrained from mixing in any State affairs. He was prepared, no doubt, to wait many years for the great change in his condition that Christina had destined for him. He was Generalissimo of the army, was given the title of Royal Highness and a decent revenue for the upkeep of his court, but Christina refused to allow him a Principality. She said it was an *Arcanum Domus Regiæ* that no land should be assigned to a hereditary Prince. This phrase was a favourite one with her when she wanted to enforce her will upon him. The Garter of the dethroned Charles II was offered to him, but Christina forbade his accepting it. " No foreigner shall put his mark on my sheep," she said. Besides, foreign orders might interfere with loyalty to his sovereign, " who should be as jealous as a husband is of the honour of his wife ". On the same principle she refused to allow him the governorship of the Swedish possessions in Germany. He was always acquiescent in these little tyrannies, and contented himself with the excellent sport on his productive island, and the rebuilding of his château, anxious above all to please his benefactress who was so powerful that she was capable of revoking the Act of Succession if he did not behave himself.

Christina temporized with her Ministers when she promised they should know at her coronation whether she would marry or not. She had not the least intention of marrying. Magnus de la Gardie had inspired her with a special aversion from Charles Gustavus, and it seems not unlikely that he had also proved to her that a close and permanent relation with any man would be odious to her peculiar nature. *Tout savoir!* Christina's curiosity about life surely did not stop short of one of its most intriguing mysteries. Whatever she may say in her Memoirs, there was nothing virginal in her temperament. She was rather a bachelor by nature and inclination. " *Libero io nacqui e vissi e morrò sciolto* " was the inscription she had engraved on a medal in later life. " Free ! " That was all that mattered.

Christina, in spite of her contempt for clothes, had a great love of pageantry, and her coronation was of a magnificence that nearly drained the coffers of Sweden quite dry. On the 14th of October, 1650, she retired from Stockholm to the de la Gardie house at Jacobstad, whence she was to make her state entry into the capital. Her host entertained her with great magnificence, and in order to supply plenty of drink for everyone, four fountains of Spanish and French wines, white and red, played throughout a day and night. It was an unfortunate year for so much splendour, for bad harvests and famine had made the plight of the peasants worse than ever.

On the 20th there was a magnificent exodus of the nobility from Stockholm to escort her to her capital. At two o'clock the procession began, led by a regiment of cavalry. There followed:

The Guards in yellow and black.

Trumpeters and drummer with silver drums.

Pages in blue and yellow velvet with silver trimmings.

Trumpeters and officers of the Court.

THE QUEEN'S CHARGER, covered with a black velvet cloth embroidered with gold.

More trumpeters and a great number of Her Majesty's gentlemen and the nobility of Livonia.

The rest of the nobility of the country.

All the Senators of the Realm each in his own carriage.

Prince Adolphus, brother to Charles Gustavus.

Ambassadors' carriages.

PRINCE CHARLES GUSTAVUS.

The Grand Equerry, who walked in front of the Queen's carriage.

THE QUEEN'S CARRIAGE, which was of black velvet covered with gold embroidery, and was surrounded by a quantity of Pages of the Chamber, halberdiers, archers, footmen who walked behind and around it.

The Queen-Mother and her suite.

All the ladies of the Court.

Twelve mules richly harnessed, and six wagons carrying the Queen's luggage.

An immense triumphal arch had been erected at the entrance of the city. Though made of wood, and covered with stuff, it had been painted to resemble stone, with battle scenes from the German war depicted, emblems and devices, and an elaborate inscription in gold letters on black, praising the greatness of the Queen and her reign. This work of art, the like of which had never been seen, cost sixteen thousand crowns.

Friday and Saturday were spent in preparations for the coronation ceremony and presentation of gifts to the Queen from her subject states and cities.

At eleven on Sunday the great coronation procession began. The Grand Treasurer carried the Golden Key; the Chancellor carried the Golden Apple; Gustav Horn, son of the great Admiral who had died, carried the Sceptre, and the Grand Constable Jacob de la Gardie, now blind, carried the Sword, led by his son, Jacques de la Gardie.

Her Majesty, in a crimson velvet car richly embroidered in gold, was surrounded by her officers, pages and halberdiers, among whom was Count Magnus de la Gardie, who carried the Royal Banner.

After some beautiful music, good long sermons were preached by the Bishop of Strengnas, her old tutor Matthaie, and the Archbishop, and then the coronation began. Christina repeated the oath word by word in a loud, clear voice after the Chancellor, and the Archbishop, taking with two fingers the precious oil from the cruse he held, anointed her head, after which he placed the crown upon it. The Grand Officers presented her with the Sword, the Sceptre, the Golden Apple and the Key. A herald cried to the people present:

" The most powerful Christina is crowned, Herself and No Other! "

After that, with Charles Gustavus, in a long robe of ermine, at her side, she sat on a throne to receive the homage of her subjects. And then in a superb triumphal chariot of gold, drawn by four white horses, she drove back to the Palace, her Treasurer scattering gold medals and money among the crowd as she went; the cannon roared, the people shouted, and nearly everyone forgot for the moment that there were such things as poverty and discontent. Perhaps in the Cathedral, Axel Oxenstierna, who loved Sweden better than himself, looking back at another coronation, may have sighed for the loss of her greatest son at so critical a moment of her history, and for the obstinate egotism of the blue-eyed little monarch perched up there with Gustavus's crown on her head. Her extravagance was dragging her country deeper and deeper into the debt from which it had never had a chance to recover since the war.

Magnus de la Gardie and his futile mission to France! There he was, brilliant and still triumphant—his Queen's banner held high aloft—his cold eye glancing at Charles Gustavus in his ermine robe. Heir to the throne Charles might be, but when would that shadow turn to substance? Husband to Christina he would never be; Magnus had seen to that. Charles was admirably disposed of, tucked away safely in his château, quietly pursuing his bucolic pleasures and buxom wenches, the prospect of his remote future keeping him on excellent behaviour. For Magnus the way was now even clearer. His marriage with a Palatine had only consolidated his position. Christina continued to caress him, and there was little fear of a rival to his own urbane charms at the Swedish Court.

It was a galling fact that Axel Oxenstierna, one of the great figures of European history, had less influence on the Queen than that pretty courtier. It was not surprising if the deep, sombre eyes of the Chancellor were turned balefully upon the young favourite. He did not know that here was only the beginning of his tragedy, that his young charge and pupil was destined to go against every principle that he had tried to teach her, that the power of Magnus de la Gardie was of the minutest importance in the sum of Christina's strange, disorganized life.

CHAPTER III

PHILOSOPHERS

CARTESIANISM was the fashion in Paris. All the leading lights in literature and society flocked to hear Descartes's new doctrines expounded. Philosophy became a more modish topic than clothes or alchemy. Automatism, geometry, medicine and morals—the dictum, "*Je pense; donc, je suis*"—were discussed in boudoirs and powder-closets, problems in the higher mathematics were handed round like *billets-doux*, and, though there was the usual display of brilliant reasoning among the real intellectuals, so much nonsense was talked elsewhere that Molière was driven to write "*Les Précieuses Ridicules*".

Descartes, "the true liberator of the spirit, the *maître des maîtres*", had himself abandoned Paris in 1629. City life was inimical to the development of his philosophical apprehension. He found seclusion necessary for the study of man's nature, the soul—and God. He did not so much live life as observe it, and that from a solitary peak. From her Northern eyrie Christina sent the philosopher a question: "When one makes a bad use of love or hate, which of these abuses is the worse?" There followed a lengthy correspondence on the subject of love, which subject she and Pierre Chanut had been fervently discussing. Descartes's contribution to the argument was mainly academic, his own experience of love having been limited to a mild passion for a little girl with a squint, in early childhood. His opinion was that love wrongly used was more dangerous than hate. After a further exchange of letters, the idea that had been at the back of Christina's mind from the first was mooted. Would Descartes visit the Swedish Court, and expound his doctrines to the eager Queen in person?

When the summons came, the philosopher was comfortably established at Egmond, in Holland. Here physics, music, mathematics and flowers occupied him to the almost total exclusion of human contacts. " I take my walk every day through the confusion of a great multitude with as much freedom and quiet as you could find in your rural avenues," he wrote to a friend from Amsterdam. The mass of correspondence that poured in from all Europe was conveyed to him by priests who acted as intermediaries. At Egmond he could practise his religion without interference; he was a Catholic. Here he could preserve his carefully guarded health, unhampered by social obligations. He ate no meat, drank little wine, and the greater part of his thinking was done in bed. His strength was never over-taxed, for he did not believe in laborious study; " a very few hours daily in thoughts which occupy the imagination, and a very few hours yearly in those which occupy the understanding—all the rest of my time is given to the relaxation of the senses and the repose of the mind."

To control in peace and quiet the thought of Europe, to pursue unchecked his enthralling investigations, this was all he asked of life. His most interesting friendship was with Princess Elizabeth, daughter of the exiled Queen of Bohemia, who lived in semi-state and great melancholy at the Hague. He occupied her mind with delightful and scarcely soluble mathematical problems, and no doubt observed the reactions (though he did not call them that) of his royal pupil to the novelty of his doctrines as keenly as he watched the struggles of the unfortunate animals he vivisected to prove that " no matter thinks; every soul of beast is matter; therefore no beast thinks ".

Descartes was not only unwilling to abandon his secret Dutch pleasaunce. He was also suspicious that this invitation might be a plot on the part of his enemies; as a Catholic and the author of a new philosophy he had reason for caution.

It was not until October, 1649, that he was persuaded to move, under the assurances of his friend Chanut and Freinsheim, the Queen's librarian. A ship was sent by Christina to convey him to Sweden, the pilot of which, when questioned by the Queen as to what manner of man he had brought with him, replied:

" Madam, I have not brought you a mere man, but a demigod."

Descartes's appearance was insignificant—he was short, his head was large and covered with untidy black hair, his voice weak, and his habit usually black and unobtrusive. For this journey he had decked himself out with unwonted care; a curled wig, elegant shoes and elaborate embroidered gloves were worn in honour of the Sibyl of the North, but this was not enough to provoke such enthusiasm. His personality must have been impressive indeed.

It was disconcerting to be asked to take part in a ballet on his arrival, but he evaded this by consenting to write some lyrics for it instead. He lodged, not in the Palace, but with his friend Chanut, where he imagined he would be the better able to pursue his own mode of life. After two interviews with Christina, he wrote to the Princess Elizabeth, who strongly disapproved of this visit:

> The generosity and majesty of the Queen in all her actions is combined with such sweetness and goodness as

> to make everyone her willing slave. She is extremely given to study, though I cannot say what she will think of my philosophy, as she knows nothing of it yet.

Descartes was not in favour of reading. Erudition was all very well for *dilettanti* and *les précieuses*, but for the true philosopher the study of nature and human life was what mattered. " These are my books," he once said to a visitor at Egmond, pointing to the bodies of animals he had dissected. The sight of Christina engrossed in the Classics depressed him. Of what use were these dead languages to a new philosophy?

Christina did not relax her studies on Descartes's account, but she showed him many marks of especial favour, even consulting him on matters of State, to the annoyance of her Swedish advisers and of the other philosophers and savants who were already gathering about her. Descartes enjoyed the company of the Queen, and so interesting did she find his philosophy that, though she exempted him from levées, which he disliked, she sought his company in *tête-à-tête* more and more. Unfortunately, the business of ruling occupied the better part of her day; she was never, even in ill-health, absent from the Senate. Then there were her studies, from which not even Descartes could lure her. So she fixed upon the uncomfortable hour of five in the morning for the exposition of Cartesianism. For any human being this would be a trial, but for Descartes it was a martyrdom. As he drove beside the river, buffeted by freezing Baltic winds in the bleak darkness long before dawn, he must have sighed for his Dutch retreat and the warm inviting bed from which he never stirred till midday. No wonder he wrote to the Princess Elizabeth, to her great delight:

> After all, in spite of my great veneration for Her

Majesty, I do not think I am likely to be detained in this country after next summer.

He was not detained as long as that. His friend Chanut fell ill of inflammation of the lungs, and Descartes nursed him back to health, but himself developed the malady, and, weakened by unwonted exposure to the severe climate and the unnatural hours he had been obliged to keep, he died on February 1, 1650.

His death stirred Europe. Christina was blamed for it, and indeed by her lack of consideration for a delicate man, she could be called indirectly responsible. Madame de Motteville said: "Instead of making men die of love for her, she makes them die of shame and despair. She caused the death of Descartes by disapproving of his philosophy." This is only one of Madame's usual exaggerations. Descartes was not the kind of person to die either of shame or despair, though Christina may have hinted that all his theories were not original, and quoted Plato.

Mademoiselle Descartes, a noted *précieuse*, friend of Mademoiselle de Scudéry and Madame de Sevigné, was moved to write a long "Relation de la Morte de M. Descartes" in prose and verse, which ends with the appearance of the philosopher to Mademoiselle de la Vigne:

Merveille de nos jours, jeune et sage Heroine,
Qui, sous les doux appas d'une beauté divine
Cachez tant de vertu, d'esprit et de sçavoir,
Ne vous étonnez pas qu'un Mort vous vienne voïr.
Si je pus autrefois, pour une jeune Reine
Dont je connoissais peu l'âme inégale et vaine,
Abandonner les lieux si fleuris et si verde,
Pour aller la chercher au pays des hivers;
Je devois bien pour vous quitter ces climats sombres
Où, loins de la lumière, errent les pales ombres.

Descartes was buried with great simplicity among the graves of children and orphans at Stockholm, and Christina erected a monument to his memory. The Abbé Huet wrote, that he visited the spot and found that the monument, instead of being of marble, as it appeared, was of painted wood. Someone had mockingly changed the inscription " *Sub hoc lapide* " to " *Sub hoc ligneo* ". Seventeen years later the body of Descartes was moved to S. Genevieve, Paris.

Descartes may be said to have inaugurated the reign of philosophers and savants at the Swedish Court. Everyone who had the slightest pretension to learning was bidden by the Queen, " *avide de sçavoir* ", as Mademoiselle Descartes describes her. From all parts they came, good and bad. Rewards were heaped upon them, gold chains, copper, and pensions without end. As a house with a chalked sign attracts tramps, so the Swedish Court became the Mecca for all sorts and conditions of scholars.

Among the really distinguished was Vossius, who came from Holland and was the greatest Greek scholar of his time. It was with him that Descartes sorrowfully observed Christina persisting in her daily classical studies. Vossius had an interesting career and was eventually made Canon of Windsor by Charles II, mainly, it was said, because he professed to believe in everything except the Bible. He was one of the worst thieves in the whole of Christina's entourage, and was believed to have stolen the priceless Codex Argenteus, a manuscript of the Gothic translation of the four Gospels made in the fourth century. This wonderful treasure was made of a papyrus stained with violet, and each letter was painted in silver or gold. It was originally found in the Benedictine abbey of Werden, Westphalia, and transferred to Prague, where it was seized by Königsmark and sent to Christina as a present. Vossius somehow got possessed of it, and at his death Magnus de la Gardie bought it and gave it to the University of Upsala, one of the few actions that can be recorded to his credit.

Nicholas Heinsius, who did not rob Christina's library, though he had ample opportunity, was sent to Italy in search of manuscripts and books. Christina urged him with encouraging letters. "You know I am curious. Satisfy my curiosity. You will be well rewarded."

Heinsius wrote from Italy: "The Italians are beginning to complain that ships are laden with the spoils of their libraries, and that all their best aids to learning are being carried away from them to the remotest North."

But Christina was insatiable. Vossius, scouring the Low Countries, France and Germany, bought on her behalf the Petau library, which Saumaise called the marrow of the manuscripts of France, for forty thousand livres. Cardinal Mazarin's library was for sale when Vossius was in Paris. He bought the best of this, and the pick of half a dozen others. The nucleus of Christina's library was a vast collection of treasures, the spoils of her father's conquests in Germany, and the final enrichment was Vossius's own library which he sold her for twenty thousand florins, on condition that he was made librarian at five thousand florins a year, with his board and lodging at Court. An admirable arrangement this, for him, of which he took full advantage, a vast quantity of Christina's books and manuscripts being found in his possession at his death.

"The royal library," wrote Huet in 1654, "is stuffed full. Four large rooms won't hold it." It was the most remarkable private library in the world. Christina's passion for owning books was matched by her love of collecting works of art of all kinds. Her taste was wide if not impeccable, and her emissaries were searching Europe for *objets d'art* of all descriptions: sculpture, pictures, engravings, medals of gold and silver, for which she had a special predilection, ivory, amber, clocks, mirrors and every possible kind of furniture came pouring in from all parts. All the noted craftsmen were bidden to the Palace; enamel-workers, engravers, wax-modellers and their like brought their wares, and went away handsomely rewarded. Dancers, singers, actors were engaged from the other end of Europe if Christina heard good reports of them. Such lavish and reckless expenditure had seldom been known, and as the Palace groaned under the cumbering masses of booty forever accumulating, Christina must have glanced apprehensively at the dwindling exchequer. How long would it last? She had enough sense to know that it could not last forever. A wild extravagance was upon her. For her honour she must spend—spend—more than any monarch had spent before her. To outshine Solomon in wisdom and glory, to have the world crying, " Great is Christina of the North ! "

It was not enough to be a great ruler. That was born in her—a gift passed on from great Gustavus I, and handed on bright and shining through her father to herself. She had proved that, since at sixteen she had sat and directed her Ministers in the Senate. They listened to her, not from deference to her sex and youth, but because she was wise in statecraft and nearly always right.

The strangest and perhaps the most interesting among Christina's collection of savants was Saumaise (Salmatius), " a man of enormous reading and no judgment ", who was lured away from the University of Leyden and lodged in the Palace. He was an exceedingly tiresome person among his fellows, domineering and arrogant. Bayle says of him, " He plunged his pen into bile of the bitterest." Maussac and Gaulmin (who presented Christina with his Oriental collection and received a gift of thirty thousand crowns in return) were once with him in the royal library in Paris, and Gaulmin said:

" I think we three could hold up our heads against all the learning in Europe," to which Saumaise replied:

" Add yourself and Maussac to the rest and I will hold my own with the lot of you."

This arrogant remark, however, may have been prompted by the extreme complacence of Gaulmin.

Christina had a genuine affection and admiration for Saumaise. She was perfectly aware that he was intolerable in his behaviour to her other guests.

" Monsieur Saumaise knows the word for ' chair ' in every language, but he hasn't learnt how to sit down on one," she said.

Doubtless he was not alone among her guests in lack of social gifts, and his learning outweighed his other shortcomings. Besides, in spite of his overbearing ways, the other side of what might be called his dual existence roused, especially in Christina, a deep, if somewhat amused pity. For if in the library he was a bitterly hated tyrant, in his home he was the victim of a subjugation most humiliating. His wife, Anne Mercier, was a dragon, a shrew, a horrible ambitious creature who by sheer malignity reduced him to a state of wretched acquiescence. So outrageous was her conduct that the whole world knew of it. Huet writes of her thus:

> I should not tell you anything of the imperious temper of Madame Saumaise if it were not already well known, and if Milton had not already written about it. She was so afraid of people putting her husband against her that she could not bear to allow anyone to see him privately. In my own experience when I have been with him at some rendezvous fixed

> by him at a certain hour away from his home so that we could converse at our leisure, his wife has never failed to arrive and break up the conversation, haughtily carrying off to the common sitting-room her poor husband, who does not dare to say a word in his defence, and contents himself with shrugging his shoulders and lifting his eyes to heaven.

Time had taught him to shrug his shoulders, merely—to lift his eyes to heaven—for peace's sake—to shut himself secure within himself from the nagging of Anne and the noise of his children. He used to work in the little common sitting-room—himself the centre of a raging whirlpool. It was not surprising that bile gathered in his pen and that his outlook was jaundiced. Ménage says of him that he was the most sociable of men, and evidently found much to like in him, but this was in early days before the poison had done its work.

To stay with such a woman, to endure for a moment, much less a lifetime, the humiliation of her odious tyranny, would seem to argue weakness of character. But habit, and above all, respectability, overcome most things. Domestic storms that sweep beyond the doors and windows of what is called home are apt to interfere with financial security. Professors must at all costs guard their home-lives from open scandal, and the University of Leyden, which prized Saumaise so dearly that when he had been in Stockholm a year Christina was told that in depriving it of him she was depriving it of the sun, would have been shocked at any deliberate change in his condition. So it was just part of life, but a very big part. When he escaped from that part of it and took up his quarters in the Palace of Stockholm, he was not allowed to forget his Anne when he donned the dreadful scarlet trappings she had designed specially for his visit to royalty. Even this horrid humiliation he did not resist, to the amusement of his sober-suited colleagues.

The Queen betook herself to his quarters at all hours, and when he was ill she delighted to " nurse " him, which consisted chiefly, from all accounts, of warming his bed—presumably with a warming-pan. Her heart must have gone out to this victim of the marriage tie, who with all his wisdom could not smooth its painful knots.

Anne was soon to follow her husband to Sweden, but he did not waste the short emancipation he enjoyed before her arrival.

One evening during his illness he was lying in bed deep in a new book reputed to be by François Beroalde, Canon of Tours, " Le Moyen de Parvenir ", a lively volume of which all Paris was talking. Whilst thus engaged he was surprised by a visit from the Queen, accompanied by Ebba Sparre. Hastily, but not hastily enough, he hid the book. Christina, ever alert, demanded its name.

" A book of somewhat risky tales, Your Majesty," he whispered, " which I was reading to while away the tedium of convalescence."

The Queen, delighted, seized the book and began reading it under her breath. Putting it into Ebba's hand, she said:

" Come, Sparre, here's a pretty book of devotions. Read this page aloud."

Ebba read a few words, then stopped short, confused.

" Go on, go on! " cried the Queen. " Read to the end! "

Ebba had to obey, while the Queen, holding her sides, watched the blushes of her favourite maid-of-honour. That much-discussed book had probably never been read under more piquant circumstances.

Christina enjoyed bizarre jokes. When she was entertaining her friends she would sometimes send for her little chorus of girls and make them sing French part-songs of outrageous impropriety, all given with artless innocence, because the singers were under the impression that they were singing devotional chants, Christina and her friends writhing with suppressed laughter.

While Saumaise was at Christina's Court his famous battle of Latin words with Milton was in full swing. The tightly-bound Saumaise must have contrasted his own lot with that of the poet, whose domestic situation, in spite of what the Italians considered his offensively strict morality, was not without inspiriting variety. His wife was immediately bored by a dull home, and he discovered that she was stupid, so they separated for a time, during which Milton wrote a treatise on divorce and cast his eye over other possible helpmeets, at the end of which time his wife went on her knees and begged to be taken back. If only Anne could be brought to her knees even for a moment!

Saumaise wrote a defence of Charles I at the instance of Charles II, who was then at the Hague. Milton replied with a "Defence of the People of England", in which, by the way, he eulogized Christina, declaring her fit to govern not only Europe, but the whole world. Since the brochure appeared while Saumaise was at Stockholm, Christina read it and was naturally enchanted by this appreciation, as no doubt Milton meant she should be, and she did not fail to let Saumaise know her high opinion of the "Defence". Milton lost his sight after he had finished this work, and Saumaise died before he could publish his "Responsio". When Milton heard that his enemy had boasted of making him lose his sight, he said:

"And I have made him lose his life."

Which shows how vindictive even an academic quarrel can make the soberest of men.

Saumaise prepared unwillingly to return to Leyden and take up once more the drudgery of his home-life. He resented the continual arrival of philosophers and savants at the Palace. He knew how much most of them were worth. There was no end to them. They flocked like birds of prey round the throne of the Sibyl, hovering about her, fighting for her favours, pouring out panegyrics with sickening ease, croaking Latin and Greek. Christina was certainly too kind to these vultures, much too indiscriminate. There were only a few men in Europe worthy of her patronage, and he, Saumaise, was the most important of them, and he was forced to leave the scene of action. Something must be done to stop the too-generous flow of her favours.

Nothing kills like ridicule, and Saumaise found a way.

CHAPTER IV

THE BARBER OF SENS

Delicate, neurotic and overworked, Christina became seriously ill in 1651. She went to Nyköping to meet her mother, who was returning in state from Germany. Marie Eleanore had long ago left Denmark; her old friend and admirer, Christian IV, had died.

Christina had had a good deal of fever in the last years, but it was on her way to Nyköping that her symptoms became alarming. At supper she fainted, and remained unconscious for hours; her pulse faded and she lay as if dead. Then for six hours she was racked with violent pain. What was there to do but bleed the patient? Scarcely any other remedy was known to the honest but ignorant physicians of the North. In spite of the pain and blood-letting, she continued her journey, and, accompanied by Charles Gustavus, arrived at Stockholm with a cheerful countenance. These serious attacks were attributed by her advisers to excess of sobriety—too much water, which perhaps was a dangerous drink in those days, and too little wine.

It was about this time that the Queen went to inspect the fleet that she was equipping in Stockholm. At one of her favourite hours, four o'clock in the morning, she was standing with Admiral Flemming on a short, narrow plank examining a new battleship, when the Admiral, excitedly pointing out to her the beauties of the new ship, fell, pulling the plank and Her Majesty into very deep water. One of her equerries, Count Steinbergh, leapt to the rescue and seized Christina by her skirt. The Admiral, who had sunk to the bottom, and no doubt on his upward journey clutching the nearest object, seized her by the petticoats too. A struggle between the two courtiers nearly lost Christina her life, but she was finally rescued by someone else, who dragged her out by her arms. Though she must have fallen in head first and swallowed a good deal of water, and have been exhausted by the struggle, her first command on being landed was to save the Admiral, who was still clinging to her skirts. She showed her usual high spirits and hardihood by making light of this episode, refusing to go to bed, and appearing at a public dinner the same day, when she delighted the company with her description of it. It does not seem to have harmed her in spite of her delicate state of nerves and general health.

It was her health that gave Saumaise his opportunity.

He produced Bourdelot.

This son of an apothecary called Michon, of Sens, which was in the neighbourhood of Saumaise's birthplace, had all the attributes necessary for a *chevalier d'industrie*; moreover, he really did know something about medicine. He inherited from his uncle, a distinguished Paris physician, his name Bourdelot, a fine collection of books and curiosities —and his profession.

He had been in Italy and boasted on his return that Pope Urban VIII had offered him a cardinal's hat if he would but stay and minister to his health, which was not unlikely, cardinal's hats having often been bestowed for less. It was at this point that his opportunity at the Swedish Court came. Gui Patin says that he himself was bidden to Sweden but refused to go, which gave Bourdelot his chance. At any rate, he arrived with very warm recommendations from Saumaise. There is not much doubt that Bourdelot was given a clear idea of the situation in Stockholm and of the necessity of turning back the tide of savants which was still pouring in from all parts. Saumaise must also be given the credit of desiring to help the Queen, for his belief in Bourdelot as a physician was genuine. Patin detested Bourdelot, but Patin was a member of the Faculté de Medicine, which was as suspicious of a free lance as any medical society to-day. He says, among other things:

> He lies nearly as much as he talks, and when he can he deceives the sick too. He brags here in good company that he was the discoverer of the circulation of the blood, and that his colleagues do all in their power to deprive him of the credit. He is a deep-dyed flatterer, grand servant of the apothecaries, and with all his fanciful bragging, a horrible liar.

This was mild for Patin, who was one of the most vitriolic haters of his day. Bourdelot continued to annoy his fellow-physicians for many years after his meteoric career at Stockholm. Among his patients were Louis XIV and the Prince de Condé.

Madame de Sevigné writes:

> I am in the hands of Bourdelot, who physics me with melon and ice, which everyone says will kill me. This idea makes me so irresolute that, though I feel myself better for what he orders me, I take it trembling.

Melon and ice! Delicious and harmless were many of

Bourdelot's remedies, and his cures sometimes appeared to be miraculous, because he was primarily a psychologist, as all successful adventurers (and doctors) are. There is no doubt that, though his character was of the lightest, he was an enthralling companion.

His effect upon Christina was immediate. She was weak and ailing when he arrived—her nerves on the rack, her constitution protesting against the outrageous way she had been overworking it. The last remedy for her ills was blood-letting. Her body was starved of sleep; she ate scarcely anything, and drank less. So indifferent was she to food that no one ever heard her express either likes or dislikes for what she ate. She had none. When she could avoid sitting down to a meal she did. State banquets, unless there was brilliant conversation, bored her, but it was naturally part of her duty, which she had never, so far, shirked, to attend many of them. On those occasions she scarcely ate.

She was not likely to die of a plethora. Yet her physicians continued to bleed her—draining the impoverished blood from her veins. Bourdelot was only just in time.

He was just in time, and Christina was immediately infatuated with him. He was, from the moment he arrived, constantly at her side, and took control of the whole situation: as her doctor he forbade visits from anyone he objected to. . The savants waited forlornly for audiences.

" No one may see Her Majesty to-day! "

The word of Bourdelot went forth. There was no gainsaying it, and the Queen was perfectly happy to see no one—not even de la Gardie, now Grand Treasurer, so long as Bourdelot was there to play with her. For now she wanted to play with a light heart—her spirit was weakened by overwork, and she surrendered contentedly to the régime Bourdelot laid down for her.

"Your Majesty needs amusement! Forget the Classics for a while and give your great brain a rest!"

This was the burden of his counsel. He himself supplied the amusement. He turned her supple mind to lighter things than dry-as-dust philosophies. He sang her Italian love-songs, his eyes half shut over the guitar he played so nimbly. If there was one thing Christina loved it was a guitar. He told her delicious tales from Paris—he discoursed of Rome, of the intriguing life there, the oranges and lemons, the warm, sunny winter days.

He taught her some splendid new oaths, of which she already had a notable collection. He filled her days with occupations in which there was not a grain of dust from heavy tomes nor a breath of stuffiness from learned beards. They invented together some enchanting new perfumes and dabbled lightly in alchemy. Christina basked in a well-being of which she had never dreamed. "Jests and ridiculous sports" were the order of the day. She realized ever more clearly as she got a keener perspective of her life as Queen—looking at it as it were through Bourdelot's eyes—how arduous and how boring it really was. The ceremonies of State, the long harangues to which she was obliged to listen, the official duties which compelled her to take a personal share in some great ceremonial observance were abhorrent to her; the range of cultivation within which her countrymen were content to confine themselves appeared to her contemptible.

This was the limit of exasperation. She had not been concerned only for her own culture; she had built colleges, endowed libraries, established a printing-press, attended debates at Upsala—had done, in fact, everything that was possible to encourage scholarship among her countrymen.

It was ungrateful work, and she was tired of it. She was not tired of learning, though she was a little tired of savants. But one could have great sport even with them. It was fun to make M. Bochart from Paris play at battledore and shuttlecock with her before a large distinguished company. Or the flute, which he had never learned. Best of all was a scene in which Meibomius, a stuffy person who had written a treatise on the music of the ancients, and Naudé, who had written another on the art of dancing, were ordered to illustrate their theories practically. Meibomius was to sing, and Naudé was to dance to his singing. As neither of these learned men had any idea of singing or dancing, and Naudé was crippled with gout, the result was excruciating, and the whole Court was convulsed with merriment at the spectacle. Meibomius, at the end of the exhibition, well aware of who was at the bottom of this joke, gave Bourdelot a resounding smack in the face, which, exciting as it was for the spectators, led to his immediate banishment from the Court.

Christina, if she ever had any sense of proportion, seems to have lost whatever shred there was of it. Bourdelot's influence was hypnotic. Her change of conduct, puzzling as it was to her Ministers, was regarded with deep apprehension by Magnus de la Gardie. It was obvious to the late favourite that his star was waning. The Queen scarcely noticed him nowadays. He went so far as to address a formal protest against Bourdelot, accusing him of slander. Bourdelot gallantly took up the challenge of this accusation, called as witnesses the people to whom he was supposed to have slandered de la Gardie, and emerged triumphant. De la Gardie's star continued to decline.

Christina and Bourdelot were soon the talk of Sweden. In fact the whole of Europe was in a very short time chattering about the queer situation up in Stockholm. Bourdelot, the apothecary's valet, first favourite! He was, of course, the Queen's lover; at any rate, he encouraged her in vicious unmentionable habits. Heaven only knew what went on when they were locked together in their laboratory, ostensibly making perfumes or seeking the philosopher's stone. And was he merely showing her, expert cook that he was, how the Italians cooked *maccheroni*?

It was not only a feast for the gossips, but the Ministers grew grave at a state of things that threatened the fair fame of the throne. If it could have been one of themselves, it would have been perhaps tolerable, but an ill-bred foreign apothecary in absolute power at Court was an outrage on decency.

Bourdelot was not the only Frenchman in attendance on Christina. There was a remarkable young man called Clairet Poisonnet, who had been in the service of the Swedish ambassador to Poland and was brought to Stockholm by his master. Bourdelot was responsible for Clairet's entering the Queen's service. He began humbly as comfiter and keeper of the linen—a simple creature, apparently, of no education, who could not read or write. It was at a masquerade that he first attracted Christina's attention. The fashionable hairdresser was also a Frenchman and his name was Champagne. This artist, spying Clairet, and seeing that he was a handsome, fresh-coloured youth with a wonderful head of his own hair, had a fancy to put him in modish feminine clothes and dress his hair in the latest fashion. The pretty masquerade made a great sensation, and Christina was so delighted with him that she kept him almost continually in this habit, until she found that besides being diverting he was gifted with rare qualities which were too good to waste. Though he could not read or write, or perhaps because he could not, he possessed a mind of unusual alertness, a genius for secrecy and faithful service, and a capacity for keeping his own counsel even in his cups.

The more he was plied with wine, as he continually was by his enemies, the more reserved he became. On the other hand, he could wring the deadliest secret out of the most seasoned spy, to such a pitch that Chanut had forbidden his servants to have anything to do with him. His memory, not having been impaired by education, was prodigious. Altogether he was a valuable creature. When there was all the trouble about Bourdelot, and Christina was anxious above all to keep on good terms with France, and possibly take refuge there if she abdicated—she must " nurse " all the alternative refuges carefully—she sent Clairet with a letter of credit between the soles of his boots to Paris, where he interviewed the Secretary of State for Foreign Affairs, and brought back his answer safely stored in his own head.

The Queen was now shameless in her complete indifference to the canons of behaviour in church. She would sit on a chair of purple velvet, leaning her head and arms on another, dreamily gazing into space, and only when the sermon was too long, as it usually was, rousing herself and rapping impatiently with her fan, or audibly playing with her two little spaniels. Bourdelot, the atheist, was accused of undermining her faith, but this is hardly fair, as she never had had the slightest respect for the faith of her father. She was, in fact, not by nature religious, though she studied the subject as eagerly as she did everything else. She was to be converted, but she was tired of the throne long before her conversion. In 1651 she had confided to Chanut her wish to abdicate, and announced it to the Senate, but the judgment of Chanut, and indeed of all her advisers, prevailed, so she acquiesced in a situation which was daily becoming more irksome.

Her interests outside her immediate circle were still and always fixed on the South. The French situation was absorbing, and she could not resist dipping her fingers into it. One of her heroes had always been the Prince de Condé, and he, aware of this, had sent a secret letter to her from the fortress of Vincennes where he was imprisoned with his brothers, the Prince de Conti and the Duc de Longueville, begging her to use her influence with the Queen Regent, Anne of Austria. This letter is dated March 26, 1650, when the war between the Frondeurs and Cardinal Mazarin's faction had reached its climax. Richelieu's reign of cruelty had been succeeded by the Sicilian Mazarin's strange policy of leniency to the people and personal greed. His hand was against the nobles and the Princes of the Blood, and this imprisonment was his last *coup*. The "Prince's Fronde" civil war which followed ended in their release a year later, partly through the ceaseless efforts of their fellow Frondeur, the Duc de Turenne, and greatly through the force of public opinion, the whole of Europe having been shaken by this high-handed act of Mazarin's towards one of France's great leaders. Anne of Austria was obliged to exile Mazarin, but he still kept a firm hand on French affairs from his retreat in Bruhl, and his remark when he retired, "Time is a good friend . . ." was fully justified, for in 1652 he was back again, more powerful than ever, and utterly indispensable in every way to the Queen Regent.

Though Christina obeyed Condé's request with alacrity, she did not have much influence in the situation. She wrote not only to the Queen Regent, but to the King, the Duc d'Orléans, the Grande Mademoiselle, Parliament and Cardinal de Retz, Mazarin's most bitter enemy. All these letters pleaded for peace, "*le bien et le repos de la France*", and she confided them to the care of a messenger who was to deliver each one personally and wait for an answer. The letter for the King was answered by Mazarin himself, who saw it in Council at St. Germain before it reached the King;

and, finding it not at all to his liking, sent a curt message to Christina that he thanked her for her goodwill, but it was not permissible for her to interfere in the differences between a sovereign and his subjects. The other notes were answered in much the same tone, but Cardinal de Retz contented himself with polite acknowledgment. He was waiting quietly for Mazarin's shoes to be empty, with the intention of stepping into them himself, and was not at the moment going to commit himself to anything.

Mazarin's action was justified on the principle that it is one of the first maxims of government that rulers should not meddle in each other's private affairs. But Christina was not likely to be discouraged by the Cardinal's attempted snub; such a gesture could only spur her into more activity. She was kept well informed of all the secret happenings in Paris by her resident, Rosenhaue, and though she did not formally interfere, she watched with deep interest the progress of events. She lost Chanut in this year, which was a great blow to her. He was sent as Minister to the Hague, and his place was taken by Picques, an inferior person whom she disliked.

Her desire for peace in France was sincere, partly because she was contemplating a visit to the Court some day in the near future, and a country at war with itself is not entertaining. Her critics asked why she was so occupied with France and so indifferent to the troubles in her own realm, which in 1650 had reached a serious climax. A bad harvest, the reckless expenditure on the Coronation, which coincided with the worst conditions known for many years, had exasperated the people. A seditious pamphlet, "Spectacles for Princes", aimed at the nobles who were bitterly hated for good reasons, warned Christina to beware of the designs of the aristocracy. She herself was never anything but beloved by the populace, in spite of her extravagance. She was a royal figure, and her decrees in their favour endeared her to her humble subjects. She was generous, but not compassionate. What she did finally to ameliorate the lot of the peasants was done greatly to annoy the nobles, and also it must be added, because her sense of justice when roused was as sane as her judgment in most things.

But she did not really care. She was deeply preoccupied with her own state of mind. More and more the trappings of the throne seemed to entangle her steps; more and more she stretched out to a fuller, freer existence. She had squeezed the juice out of ruling Sweden, and the skin was very dry, ready to be cast away. Though her attempt was frustrated in 1651, only a year after her coronation, by the dismay of the Senate when she announced her intention, she never for a moment abandoned it. She was, no doubt, flattered and touched by the pleadings of the delegation that waited upon her after the five-hour debate in the Senate. All its members, and all the notables present, joined in entreating her not to desert the throne. Oxenstierna, sober, undemonstrative man, was moved to tears. He went so far as to declare that if she carried out her threat, he and the chief officers of the State would resign their positions and leave Sweden to her fate, more as a demonstration to posterity that they had not encouraged her in a step so fatal to the realm. It is most unlikely that he or any of his colleagues would have carried out this threat, but he rightly judged that Christina would be deeply affected by such a menace to the well-being of Sweden. She gave in, and Charles Gustavus, who had tactfully joined in the chorus of dissent, saw the crown waved in front of his eyes and snatched away again without an outward sign of dismay.

Christina might well have said to her Ministers:

"How can I satisfy you? Whatever I do seems to shock you. I fill the Palace with philosophers and savants, and you remonstrate with me for spending so much on their pensions and presents. Then when I get tired of them and their dowdy inevitable wives, and find myself more amused with Bourdelot, you raise a storm and accuse me of lightness, extravagance, vice, and goodness knows what—behaviour unworthy of the Queen of a great country. Then when I offer to relieve you of my presence on the throne, you raise the biggest storm of all, and assure me that Sweden will be ruined if I abdicate. Whatever I do it seems Sweden will be ruined."

Christina must stay, but Bourdelot must go. That was the burden of everyone's thoughts and desires round about the Court. The clergy, too, were horrified. Her behaviour in church—it was really scandalous, and that villainous atheist was surely partly responsible. They forgot that Christina had never been remarkable for piety at any time. All they knew was that the piety of the people would be seriously undermined if the Queen set such an unhappy example of levity at public worship in the House of God. For some reason the heads of the Church did not feel themselves called upon to remonstrate with her. They deputed, of all people, the Queen-Mother, who was living in comparative obscurity as near to her daughter as she dared.

Marie Eleanore therefore administered at great length the reproaches and admonitions with regard to Bourdelot that seemed to be appropriate.

Christina listened in an embarrassing silence, the blue eyes gazing fixedly. Marie Eleanore began to stumble under that cold, comprehending gaze.

At last Christina interrupted her.

"Leave these matters to the priests, my dear Mother. I know quite well who has sent you, and I will give them good reason to regret their interference."

Marie Eleanore, as usual, burst into tears and retired. Christina, on being told six hours later that nothing could stop her weeping, said that she had brought it on herself, but was finally persuaded to go and see her mother. She talked of anything but the cause of the trouble, and the result of their little conversation was that the Queen-Mother retired to Nyköping.

It seems unlikely that a man of such light character as Bourdelot could have any but a negative influence on Christina's faith. He certainly influenced her mode of life to such an extent that she never went back to the dull paths of duty that she had tried to follow before her breakdown in health and his arrival on the scene. But Chanut and Descartes were the first to light the torch of Catholicism. It flickered very faintly at the beginning, and even its faint flickerings were regarded with misgiving by Christina herself. This is the only explanation, unless she was a monster of insincerity, of her attitude towards the Landgrave of Hesse when she heard that he was intending to join the Roman Church. She wrote him a strong letter:

> Since I am of a third religion which, having found the Truth, has disregarded their (Lutheran) opinions, which it has rejected as false, it is right that I should speak as a neutral person, who will only touch upon a single point which you must appreciate; it is honour that I would wish to insist upon. Surely you know how those who change are hated by those from whose sentiments they turn away, and don't you know, from many illustrious examples, that they are distrusted even by those whose ranks they join? Think, if you please, how important to the reputation of a Prince is the opinion held of his constancy, and be sure you do a great wrong to your own, if you make so grave a

mistake. When you have considered the circumstances I have mentioned, I feel sure you will change your mind.

As this letter was written as late as 1652, when Christina was already in communication with Rome, the only explanation is that she was, as it were, talking to herself, and trying to resist the impulse that was carrying her with ever-gathering force, right out into the open. She longed for freedom and emancipation from the tedium of ruling a people she no longer loved, the shedding of responsibilities no longer endurable. The fact was ever more apparent that she was irresistibly drawn to the South; that she was enamoured of the Latin temperament, and in consequence turned almost with loathing from the crude directness of her countrymen. When a Northern woman loses her head over a Latin she seldom finds it again. In the case of Christina it was not one man at this period—it was a whole race that had captured her heart. Bourdelot, a Latin if ever there was one, was the first of a long procession of foreign favourites, and it will be seen that they were true to type, till the great one arrived.

It was a nation that Christina loved: it was Italy for whose soil she longed. She dreamed of orange groves, of winter sun, of a salon that should eclipse all other salons, where she could talk on equal terms with the great minds of the time, herself, freed from the trammels of a throne, shining by virtue of her own fine gifts; the lodestar of European culture, not surrounded as at Stockholm by needy sycophants, but by the cream of civilization.

In 1651 Don Giuseppe Pinto Pereira arrived in Sweden as Portuguese Ambassador. As he knew no Latin, he could only communicate with Christina through his secretary, who acted as interpreter. This secretary falling ill, the duty of interpreter fell upon the Ambassador's confessor, Macedo, a

Jesuit. During an audience the confessor was electrified by Christina's announcement in Latin that she wished to consult with someone of his profession, but that such absolute secrecy must be observed that no letters must pass. The Jesuit managed to conceal his emotion at this amazing communication, and the audience was concluded without Pereira suspecting anything. Other audiences of the same exciting nature followed, and then Macedo announced that the air of Sweden did not suit him and begged to be given his *congé*. The Ambassador refused, but Macedo took French leave. When Pereira asked Christina's permission to have him followed and brought back, she replied that she could not allow anyone who found Sweden unhealthy to be forced to remain.

Macedo sped to Rome with the news. The General of the Company of Jesus lost no time in dispatching two zealous missionaries, Francesco Malines, professor of theology at Turin, and Paul Casati, professor of mathematics in Rome. They arrived as Italian gentlemen of leisure and were presented at Court in the usual way. Christina soon guessed who they were, and asked one of them in an aside if they had letters for her. A nod was enough. Christina was delighted. This was one of the most exciting intrigues she had yet enjoyed. If the Swedes knew what these two dark gentlemen portended! If the Chancellor could guess what went on at the private audiences of these pleasant Italian travellers!

As might be imagined, the task of the two instructors was not an easy one. Christina soon proved that she knew as much about theology as they did, and every point was argued with such ruthless logic by the royal pupil that they began to lose courage. At last, after having reduced them both to a state of bewilderment and despair, she suddenly said:

" Perhaps, after all, I am nearer to becoming a Catholic than you guess."

" At this," says Casati, " we were like men raised from the dead."

Then followed long discussions. She suggested that after her conversion she should take the sacrament in the Lutheran church once a year. On this point her advisers were quite clear. The Pope would never consent to that.

" In that case," she declared, " I must renounce the throne."

Her way was clear; here was a case of conscience!

Renunciation of the throne for Religion's sake! Impressive enough the Sibyl of the North turning from the faith for which her father died. But what would not Rome think of a young queen who renounced all to follow God? At the same time, her people must not know of her whole resolve until her affairs were well established. The shock of her abdication would be enough for them. There was her income to be considered. A great deal of tact would be necessary to induce the States to grant her a revenue equal to her needs. She knew pretty well all about the financial condition of Sweden, which had hardly recovered from the expenses of her coronation, and was not likely to be enthusiastic about financing an absent queen, least of all a Papist. A strong mind and an indomitable purpose were necessary to override any misgivings that might be lurking in her thoughts as to the honesty and justice of her demands upon the realm she was deserting. A pretty hard head was needed to carry off what might easily be described as a piece of sharp practice against her people.

The two emissaries from Rome having departed, Don Antonio Pimentelli de Parada, Envoy Extraordinary from the King of Spain, helped to keep alight the torch lit by Chanut. This courtly diplomat arrived at the Swedish

Court in 1652, and may be said to have overlapped Bourdelot in the Queen's good graces. She was instantly attracted to the suave Southerner, who opened his career at once with a pretty piece of diplomacy.

When Christina received him in formal audience, seated upon her chair of state, he approached her, gave a profound obeisance and retired hurriedly without uttering a word. Christina found this behaviour delightfully provocative, and readily consented to another audience. He then declared that he had been so overcome by the splendour and greatness of Her Majesty that he was tongue-tied, and could do no more than bow and retire. Here was the kind of flattery, spoken with passionate sincerity, which Christina enjoyed, and from that moment began a very pleasant and exceedingly close friendship with Spain's Envoy. So close that the French Court, hearing of it, began to get anxious. Christina was flirting with Spain now. That would never do.

The development was considered so serious that Chanut was ordered to visit Stockholm and inform on the situation. His report was reassuring. Christina was amusing herself with Pimentelli, whom she found very good company. That was all. Bourdelot's day was over. The Queen yielded with a good grace to her subjects' entreaties to be rid of him. He had served his purpose, and now Pimentelli was here, who was, after all, equally amusing and a man of quality as well. Bourdelot went to Paris and opened his successful career there as a fashionable physician.

" Master Bourdelot rides in a chair followed by four equerries. He declares that he has performed miracles in Sweden," says Patin.

Well, from one point of view, perhaps he had.

Christina wasted no time in sentimental regrets for her favourites or for anything else in those days. Finding a letter from Bourdelot in a packet that arrived from France, she put it to her nose, and then held it out to a lady-in-waiting to smell, crying:

"Ha! It stinks of medicine!"

She threw it on the fire without reading it.

So ended the reign of the Barber of Sens.

CHAPTER V

THE ORDER OF AMARANTA

" Dolce nella memoria " was the motto engraved on the Order of Amaranta which Christina founded in 1653. There were thirty members, fifteen ladies and fifteen knights, with the Queen at the head of them all. There is no list of membership, but among the knights and ladies were the King of Poland, Charles Gustavus and his brother Adolphus, the Landgrave of Hesse, a few German Princes, the de la Gardie family, Count Dohna and Count Tott, both devoted to Christina, and the latter a special favourite of hers, " a civil, handsome young courtier, of good parts and much of the French mode ", says Whitelock.

History does not say who were the ladies chosen by Christina, but no doubt they were amusing and handsome, and certainly Ebba Sparre was among them. Unwillingly Christina had consented to the marriage of Ebba. She was now the wife of Jacob de la Gardie, and known as the beautiful Countess. Among the Knights of the Order were Count Montecuculi from the Court of Austria, and Don Antonio de la Cueva from the Court of Spain, both of whom accompanied Christina on her travels later on. A striking pair were Count Corfiz Ulfeld from Denmark and Radzieiowski, late Chancellor of Poland. These were refugees from their own countries. Count Ulfeld had married

Leonora Christina, one of the left-handed daughters[1] of his King, Christian IV, hero of the battle of Kolberger Heide, and had been Grand Master of the Danish Court, and undisputed leader of the Danish aristocracy with his gifted wife, till the death of Christian, whom Sophie Amalie, the jealous, ambitious consort of his successor, Frederick III, plotted so effectively against that they were obliged to flee the country, the Princess disguised as a page. This heroic lady spent twenty-two years in prison after her husband's death, the victim of persecution by his enemies and of the bitter animosity of Sophie Amalie. Christina took the interesting couple under her protection, at the same time that Radzieiowski, finding Poland too hot for him, had picked on Sweden as his safest refuge.

Both men were daring and imaginative intriguers, and Christina spent a great deal more time than her Ministers liked in their company; it was said bitterly that she divided her attentions between them and Antonio Pimentelli. Certainly the refugees were both trying to persuade her to go to war with their respective countries for motives of their own, and certainly Christina enjoyed the piquancy of the situation, especially when she found them also intriguing against each other, Radzieiowski having betrayed to Denmark Ulfeld's designs, in order at least to delay things in that quarter, while his own plans were maturing. Apart from this both were men of wit and understanding, Ulfeld being especially notable for his profound knowledge of statecraft and his " facetious conversation ", says Whitelock.

The Order of Amaranta was inaugurated with a splendid ballet called " The Feast of the Gods ", followed by supper. The gods, it should be noted, were chiefly

[1] *i.e.* daughter of second wife whose children cannot inherit if there is issue of the first wife.

foreigners. Pimentelli was a glorious Mars, Ulfeld was Jupiter, and Radzieiowski set the pace of the party by being pushed in on a barrel as Bacchus, drinking out of a huge tankard. Magnus de la Gardie, whose banishment at this time was only a small cloud on the horizon, was Apollo to the life. Christina herself, as Amaranta, the Immortal One, wore a magnificent gown covered with diamonds. The rest of the courtiers were shepherds and shepherdesses and waited on the gods. A song, with "*Vive Amaranta*" as its refrain, was sung at intervals throughout the banquet. Then followed brawls and French dancing, in which Christina was always the most spirited lady present, and, half-way through the evening, she ordered everyone to cast aside his disguise, whether of god or mortal. She herself made her attendants cut the diamonds from her Amaranta gown before she disrobed. These she distributed among her guests. But to Antonio Pimentelli she gave a wonderful diamond ring.

They danced till five in the morning, and it was the success of this gallant evening that encouraged Christina to found the order. The motto for these knights and ladies was to be *Semper idem*. They swore to follow Virtue and Honour. They also swore, if unmarried, to remain so. *Semper idem!* The Order had a short life, so perhaps the vow was kept.

The insignia which Christina designed was costly and gorgeous. It was of gold thickly set with diamonds, the device a laurel wreath with two "A's" entwined in the centre. It was attached with a bright red taffeta scarf fringed with silver, tied round the left shoulder. The ladies wore it under the left breast, tied also with crimson taffeta. There was some delay in the distribution of this decoration, but Christina wore hers almost incessantly from the first moment. There were many theories as to the significance

COUNT FRANCESCO SANTINELLI

of the entwined " A's ". The simplest is that they represented the first and last letters of Amaranta, but the double coincidence of the town of Amaranta being the birthplace of Pimentelli and his Christian name being Antonio was too much for the gossips to resist. The Don was now nearly as indispensable to the Queen as Bourdelot had been, and in spite of his superior estate, he became equally unpopular. Christina yielded more easily to the urgency of her advisers than in the case of the doctor, and the Spaniard was given his *congé*. At his last audience he was pale and speechless—another bit of play-acting in the opinion of those present.

He sailed from Gothenburg, and after two or three days of tempest his vessel was obliged to put about and return to port. Pimentelli did not wait for a favourable wind, but regarding the storm as an act of God, he posted back to the Court as fast as possible, where Christina received him with unfeigned delight. He was now established more firmly than ever, and when the Court moved to Upsala on account of plague in Stockholm, he was lodged in apartments so close to the Queen's that when his carriage was waiting for him, the horses attached to it were in front of her grand staircase.

The Castle at Upsala, built of plastered brick on the top of a hill, looked down on the Cathedral City and a fair countryside, with the river Sale running at the foot of the hill and emptying itself into a lake. The old Upsala, about two miles north of the present city, was famous early in history for its magnificent temple to Thor, Odin and Frey. On this site was built the first Christian cathedral in 1100. It was destroyed by fire. The archiepiscopal see was moved to the present Upsala, and another cathedral built. The city became a great episcopal capital, where kings were crowned. Gustavus

Vasa founded the Castle in 1548, but it was never really finished. In Christina's time only two sides of the four-square building were completed, but it was of noble design and full of spacious apartments. The Queen's garden was a wretched, neglected place of four or five acres surrounded by post and rails, with nothing but a few hedges which began to get green after the thaw in May, no trees and few flowers but ordinary tulips. The climate did not encourage the planting of fruit trees or shrubs.

In 1567 the Castle had been the scene of a horrible outrage when the demented Eric XIV had three members of the great Sture family and two other noblemen put brutally to death on the pretext that they were traitors. This strange Prince, described as very handsome, marvellously accomplished and speaking many languages, amateur of music and mathematician, was the son of Gustavus by his first wife, Catherine of Saxe Lauenberg, and was therefore a great-uncle of Christina's. There were a good many points in common between them. That murder at the Castle—something of the same callousness was seen at Fontainebleau—years later.

But here was the Court, established at Upsala, awaiting with some excitement the arrival of Bulstrode Whitelock, Ambassador from the Commonwealth of England. It was winter-time, and in the cold, short days few people stirred out if they could help it. But when the sun shone and the bitter Baltic wind was still, the streets were jingling with sleigh-bells.

On some glittering frosty day Christina would flash by in her little sled, drawn by a big trotting horse gaily plumed and covered with silver bells, one of her gallants standing behind her and holding the reins. A dozen or so of her ladies would come jingling after her, each with her gallant, all in gay attire, their plumes flying, the brightly painted little sleds skimming along the white ground—bells and laughter and bright colours.

Magnus de la Gardie plunged himself deeper into disgrace with Christina at this time by another ridiculous plot to retrieve his position, involving the Queen's Equerry Steinbergh, whom he accused of having made mischief. He might have known that Christina would sift this calumny to the bottom, and it was soon proved that Steinbergh was quite innocent, but naturally sufficiently annoyed to take the matter further, and, on his demanding of de la Gardie from whom he had the slander, the latter, after much hesitation, declared that Schlippenberg, the Grand Seneschal at Stockholm, was responsible. Worse and worse! The Queen summoned all three men to appear before her, with the result that de la Gardie was completely discredited. Later in the day he sent to Christina asking to be allowed to retire to his country seat, begging her to deny Schlippenberg the Court, and to avoid speaking of the affair to his own disadvantage.

Christina haughtily replied that she not only allowed him, but ordered him to leave town, to go where he chose so long as it was not to her Court; that she could not think of using Schlippenberg as he suggested, and as to the third demand—she could feel for him nothing but pity for his self-inflicted misfortune. Even yet Magnus approached her again; this time with a letter. As she read it, she murmured several times " Poor Count! " and sent him a long reply, some of which is worth quoting:

> SIR,—As you wish to see me again after your disgrace, I must tell you how opposed this wish is to your advantage, and I write this letter to remind you of the reasons which prevent me from acceding to it, and to convince you, too, that the interview is useless

to your peace of mind. It is not for me to bring remedies for your misfortunes; it is to yourself you must look to repair your honour. What can I do except pity and blame you? The friendship I had for you compels me to do both; and however much I may have indulged you in the past, I cannot, with any sincerity, pardon you the crime you have committed against yourself. Do not imagine that I am angry with you--I assure you I am not. I can now do nothing but pity you, which can do you no good, since you have shown yourself indifferent to my friendship. You are unworthy by your own confession, and you have yourself pronounced the decree of your banishment in the sight of several persons of rank who were present. I have confirmed this decree because I found it just, and I am not ready to undo it, as you seem to suppose. After what you have done and suffered, do you dare to show yourself to me? I am ashamed to think of the many base actions you have stooped to. . . . In this unfortunate affair, no spark of magnanimity or generosity has appeared in your conduct. Were I capable of repentance I should regret ever having made a friendship with so feeble a soul as yours; but this weakness is unworthy of me, and, having always acted as reason dictated on my own impulse I ought not to blame the veil I have thrown over the course of events. I would have preserved this all my life had not your imprudence compelled me to declare myself against you. Honour compels me to do it openly, and justice forces it upon me. I have done too much for you these nine years, in always blindly taking your part against all. But now that you abandon your dearest interests, I am released from all further care of them. You have yourself betrayed a secret which I had resolved to keep all my life, by showing that you were unworthy of the fortune I built up for you. If you are determined to hear my reproaches you can come to me; I consent on this condition. But do not hope that tears or entreaties will ever force me to yield a hair's breadth. The only favour I can do for you is to remember you little and speak of you less; being determined never to mention you except to blame you. . . . Remember that you are yourself to blame for what has occurred to your disgrace, and that I am just towards you as I always will be for all the world.

CHRISTINA.

UPSALA,
December 5, 1653.

The phrase about the betrayed secret has been interpreted by some as referring to the private relations between Christina and her favourite. It seems more likely to imply simply the secret of his unworthiness of which she had always been conscious, and had tried to conceal from the world, but which was now too clearly displayed, to his undoing and her own humiliation. There were no secrets otherwise that he was likely to have betrayed. The world considered him her lover—no doubt he boasted of being so—the mystery of their relationship was never revealed.

Magnus, amazingly, still held on, even after that crushing letter, and pleaded through every channel he could find for reinstalment in her good graces. He even approached his old enemy the Chancellor, Oxenstierna, whereupon the Chancellor, with grim humour, sent the retort, that " he doted, being already in his second childhood, and no longer capable of giving counsel ", a quotation from de la Gardie himself. Nothing moved Christina. Her mind once made up was hard to alter, and Magnus retired from the contest, a bitter enemy, awaiting his time to strike.

The sober Whitelock set out with his embassy from London on the Lord's Day, November 6, 1653. The *Phœnix*, the *Adventurer*, the *Elizabeth*, the *Fortune*, a State " Catch " and a private man-o'-war commanded by a bold fighting seaman, Captain Welsh, attended the *Hope*, which conveyed Whitelock, two of his sons and some of his suite. The *Adventurer* had over thirty horses on board. At the Nore, in the mouth of the Thames, the convoy was held up by contrary winds, and Whitelock had the satisfaction of hearing the news, carried in haste by wherrymen, that his dear third wife had been safely delivered of his thirteenth child, a son. As soon as this news had been received the wind changed and the voyage began in earnest, Whitelock praising God for His blessings. There followed seven days of violent and dangerous adventure, including an encounter with Dutch ships, a few shots, but a friendly finish, wild storms and a great deal of sea-sickness for nearly everybody but the Ambassador himself, who " held well ".

They disembarked at Gothenburg, the seaport founded with immense foresight by Gustavus Adolphus, and built by Dutch settlers, which became one of the great ports of the world, and is now the key to Sweden's prosperity. Here they were received with due pomp and ceremony, but though the relief of being on land must have been great, their discomforts were not over, for after a short time spent in Gothenburg, there followed a fortnight's hard travelling on the road, with straw beds for most of the company at their stopping-places, and food consisting often of dead cows. The last three days of their journey were spent in the vast, sweet-scented forest of Valterd,[1] three hundred

[1] This forest is now extinct.

miles long and seventy miles broad, of ash and oak, firs and birches, full of wolves, bears and other wild beasts. Here, when they came to a burgh, they had better food, pork and hares, and a little bird called a yerpen, more delicate than a partridge.

When within a mile of Upsala, the embassy prepared for the arrival of Vanderlin, the Queen's Master of Ceremonies, and the pages, lackeys, and the rest put on their liveries. Whitelock complains that Vanderlin arrived in careless garb, but this lack of respect was no doubt soon forgotten in the sight of the Queen's *carosse du corps* sent to convey him, which was of green velvet inside and out, richly laced with broad silver laces and fringed, with six white horses, and twenty of the Queen's lackeys in blue and silver, in attendance. There were eighteen coaches with six horses, and many gentlemen on horseback. Great crowds watched the procession, which was nearly as impressive as Whitelock could have wished, and he was conducted to the best house in the town, which he was glad to know was second in importance only to the Castle. It had been prepared specially for him, and by the Queen's orders hung with some of her most beautiful tapestries.

This was all very satisfactory, and as near as possible worthy of his exalted station and the vast importance of his mission. No one ever took himself more seriously than Whitelock, and, his excellent diary being written in the third person, he could extol himself and his own right-doing without self-consciousness whenever it was necessary, and it continually was.

The first person of distinction to send a greeting to the English Ambassador was Don Antonio Pimentelli, and Whitelock was not long in discovering that the Spanish Envoy was indeed one of the most important people to cultivate, while Pimentelli had no doubt from the first of the expediency of friendship with the Commonwealth Ambassador.

For his first audience with Christina, Whitelock was brilliantly accompanied by his gentlemen in their richest garments, and every man with his sword at his side. But the Ambassador himself was plain though extraordinarily rich in a habit of fine black English cloth, the cloak lined with the same cloth, and " both set with very fine diamond buttons; his hat-band of diamonds answerable; and all of the value of £1,000 ".

He found the Queen sitting on her crimson velvet chair of state, surrounded by a great company. He was probably taken aback by her unceremonious attire, which was of plain grey stuff, with a man's jacket, ruffled cuffs, and a black velvet cap lined with sable, which she took off whenever Whitelock uncovered. She wore the Order of Amaranta.

While he was speaking his address in English, which was interpreted into Swedish, she gazed fixedly in his face, a disturbing habit of hers. But Whitelock flatters himself that it would take more than that to daunt him. At the end she was silent for a pretty while. He had spoken with feeling of the Protestant cause, and of its defence by her father, Gustavus Adolphus, of blessed memory. Did her mind for one moment flinch at the thought of that King, and all he had fought and died for? After the short silence she advanced, and " with a countenance and gesture full of confidence, spirit and majesty, yet mixed with great civility and good grace ", she replied in Swedish, which was translated into English, and she did not mention the Protestant cause. After this ceremonial audience they always conversed in French, Christina, with all her languages, having no English.

The commercial alliance between the Commonwealth

and Sweden, which was the object of Whitelock's embassy, was long in the making. The Chancellor was cautious from the first, but when the unexpected news came of the change of government in England, and Cromwell became supreme Governor and Protector, the progress of events was again checked because of doubts as to the validity of the Ambassador's credentials under the new régime. After he had satisfied everyone upon this point with new documents arrived from England, there were still, he felt, unaccountable delays, which kept him in Upsala nearly four months. During this time the Queen treated him with great friendliness, giving him many private audiences, and evidently enjoying his ponderous " drolling ". At the first private audience they walked up and down the room for two hours in conversation. Whitelock, who was lame, found that he was very weary, " yet at the same time in discourse with such a Princess, and upon such high matters (like a wounded man when he is hot), he felt not the pain, but felt it afterwards ". After this Christina always called for stools, and they sat discussing everything under the sun, Christina being prone to get away from the main object of their meeting as much as possible. But when the Alliance was discussed she seldom failed to insist upon the advantage of bringing Spain into it, and here the influence of Pimentelli was obvious even to Whitelock. Christina was as much concerned for Spain as she was for Sweden, perhaps more so; but most of all, as will be seen later, she was concerned for herself.

One day she sent for Whitelock, and after a long discussion upon the Protestant religion, she, to change the subject, asked how he communicated secretly with his superiors in England. He explained the invisible ink he made himself. Two glasses of water were left with the Secretary of the Council, one to write with and the other to pour over Whitelock's letters when they arrived, when the blank page became a sheet of clearly written script. Then suddenly:

THE QUEEN. What huge dog is this?

WHITELOCK. It is an English mastiff, which I brought with me. It seems it is broke loose, and followed me even to this place.

THE QUEEN. Is he gentle and well-conditioned?

WHITELOCK. The more courage they have, the more gentle they are; this is both. Your Majesty may stroke him.

THE QUEEN. I have heard of the fierceness of these dogs; this is very gentle.

WHITELOCK. They are very gentle unless provoked, and of a generous kind: no creature hath more mettle or faithfulness than they have.

THE QUEEN. Is it your dog?

WHITELOCK. I cannot tell; some of my people told me that one Mr. Peters sent it for a present to the Queen.

THE QUEEN. Who is that Mr. Peters?

WHITELOCK. A Minister, and great servant to the Parliament.

THE QUEEN. That Mr. Peters sent me a letter.

WHITELOCK. He is a great admirer of Your Majesty, but to presume to send a letter or a dog for a present to a Queen, I thought above him, and not fit to be offered to Your Majesty.

THE QUEEN. I have many letters from private persons. His letter and the dog do belong to me, and are my goods, and I will have them.

WHITELOCK. Your Majesty commands in chief, and all ought to obey you, and so will I, not only as to the letter and dog, but likewise as to another part of his present, a great English cheese of his country making.

THE QUEEN. I do kindly accept them from him, and see that you send my goods to me.

WHITELOCK. I will not fail to obey Your Majesty.

They parted "in much drollery" and the Queen was delighted with the English cheese. Whitelock's stratagem to bring the dog to her notice was crowned with success but it needed no diplomacy on his part to dispose of the English horses he had brought over with him. Christina had her eye on them from the first. In fact, they made as much impression generally as the Ambassador himself. The Swedish horses were a small nag-like breed, and though the Queen and some of the nobles kept a few large and handsome animals, they did not compare with those that Whitelock brought out of England. The first tentative came from Prince Adolphus at his first visit, who praised them so highly, and stressed so much the danger of a sea voyage to them, that Whitelock was convinced he desired a couple or so for himself. But Whitelock was not so young a courtier as to pass the compliment of their being at His Highness's service, lest he might be taken at his word. However, one day, after a discourse on hunting, the Queen herself delivered a broad hint that could not be misunderstood. She thought, she said, of sending to England for horses, whereupon Whitelock, in duty bound, assured her that if she had a liking for any of his they were at her disposal. Baron Steinbergh, Master of the Horse, was asked a few days later to bring to the Queen's notice that Whitelock was making her a small present of three saddle-horses. They were brought to the Castle and walked up and down while the Queen stood at a window for a great while judging their paces. Nothing but the snow hindered her from mounting them immediately. They were of excellent shape and mettle.

But this was not enough for Christina. She had set her heart on the splendid team of black horses which made such a stir when Whitelock went abroad in his coach. She felt that they were destined to carry her on her journey to the South. The South!

She was right, for though Whitelock was most unwilling to part with them, in the end she got them, and Prince Charles Gustavus had the other team of brilliant bays. The Chancellor was presented with a " strong, well-paced English pad nag ", and several geldings were distributed as the Queen decided among her gentlemen, including Tott and Steinbergh. Whitelock had to borrow horses for his return journey.

CHAPTER VI

ABDICATION, 1654

THE Commonwealth Ambassador, puzzled but ignorant of the upheaval that was threatening Sweden, persevered conscientiously in his mission, cultivating the right people, lecturing his suite on the folly of late nights, the evil of carousing and the sacred duty of Lord's Day observance, and getting a little impatient of the Chancellor Oxenstierna's procrastination. His audiences with the Queen were frequent, and it was at one of these that he complained of the difficulties he had with the Chancellor. Knowing well the reason for this, she listened and questioned him for a while; then drew her stool nearer to him and said:

"I shall surprise you with something which I intend to communicate to you; but it must be under secrecy."

"Madam, we that have been versed in the affairs of England do not use to be surprised with the discourse of a young lady. . . ."

"I have great confidence in your honour and judgment, and therefore, though you are a stranger, I shall acquaint you with a business of the greatest consequence to me in the world, and which I have not communicated to any creature; nor would I have you to tell anyone of it—no, not your General, till you come to see him; and in this business I desire your counsel."

"Your Majesty does me in this the greatest honour

imaginable, and your confidence in me I shall not, by the grace of God, deceive in the least measure . . . and wherein Your Majesty shall judge my counsel worth your receiving, I shall give it with all sincerity, and according to the best of my poor capacity."

"Sir, it is this. I have it in my thoughts and resolution to quit the crown of Sweden, and to retire myself unto a private life, as much more suitable to my contentment than the great cares and troubles attending upon the government of my kingdom."

The Punchinello secret was out.

"I am sorry to hear Your Majesty call it a resolution; and if anything would surprise a man, to hear such a resolution from a lady of your parts, power and judgment, would do it. But I suppose Your Majesty is pleased only to droll with your humble servant."

"I speak you the truth of my intentions; and had it not been for your coming hither, which caused me to defer my resolution, probably it might have been done before this time."

Whitelock remonstrated warmly against the project, and asked her if she could forsake her people that loved her.

"It is my love to the people which causeth me to think of providing a better governor for them than a poor woman can be, and it is somewhat of love to myself, to please my own fancy by private retirement."

Christina could be humble when it suited her.

After much improving discourse on both sides, the practical Whitelock said:

"Madam, let me humbly advise you, if any such thing should be, as I hope it will not, to reserve that country in your possession out of which your reserved revenue shall be issued; for when money is to be paid out of a prince's treasury, it is not always ready and certain."

Prophetic Whitelock!

Christina replied:

" The Prince Palatine is full of justice and honour; but I like your counsel well, and shall follow it, and advise further with you in it."

Whitelock went on:

" Suppose, Madam, as the worst must be cast, that by some exigencies or troubles your lessened revenues should not be answered and paid to supply your own occasions. You that have been mistress of the whole revenue of this Crown, and of so noble and bountiful heart as you have, how can you bear the abridging of it, or, it may be, the necessary supplies for yourself and your servants to be wanting to your quality? "

" In case of such exigencies, notwithstanding my quality, I can content myself with very little; and for servants, with a lackey and a chambermaid."

The Chancellor's tardiness was explained. He was trying to hold off the final stages of the Alliance until this period of transition was over and the Prince on the throne. Besides, he was much engaged, sadly, on the business of the Queen, whose decision he now knew to be irrevocable. He was a sick old man, though still active at the head of affairs.

Soon after this audience the Queen invited Whitelock to come and hear some music, when some excellent Italian singers and a French lady, Madame de Bar, and her brother amused the company with music " very rare ". It was a diverting evening. Montecuculi from the Court of Austria was there. Among the ladies was Ebba Sparre " the beautiful Countess ". The Queen brought her to Whitelock.

" Discourse with this lady, my bed-fellow, and tell me if her inside be not as beautiful as her outside."

Whitelock gladly tested the quality of the lovely lady's soul, while Christina seized her gloves and tore them in four pieces, dividing them between Pimentelli, the Italians and Count Tott. Whitelock gallantly responded to this with a present next day to Ebba of a dozen pairs of English white gloves, much prized among the fair sex.

Everything was now in train for Christina's abdication. It was quite obvious to everyone around her that all business of the Crown was odious to her. When the secretaries came to her with papers to sign, she cried:

" When I see these people it's like seeing the devil. . . . I want to give up government to one who has strength enough for it. The King of Sweden should be able to lead his armies."

This was ever her modest cry. In her heart she was sure she could lead an army as well as anyone else, but just now she was not going to admit it.

Pimentelli was again dismissed a month or so before her abdication. She followed him with letters full of violent expressions of affection, which were opened and read by various people *en route*, and a M. Borsel, writing to a M. de Witt in Paris, declares that if he did not know the virtue of the Queen, one might arrive at the false impression that the particular letter which M. Borsel had had the honour of reading was prompted by *un amour tout charnel.* The fact was that Pimentelli was not dismissed as far as Christina was concerned, but was engaged on important business for her in Flanders.

The Whitelock affair was at last settling itself, and, as soon as Christina was assured that the alliance between England and Sweden was concluded, she sent for Whitelock and suggested a secret article by which, if Sweden neglected its obligations to her, the Protector should not be bound by the treaty. Whitelock was not in favour of this—saw, naturally, little advantage to his own country in it, but assured the Queen that as the Protector was a great maintainer of justice and honour, he could be depended upon to be a true friend to her in any difficulties that should come to her.

"Wherewith, poor lady, she seemed much comforted, having brought her affairs to so low an ebb as this was."

Yes, this was where Christina's doubts were deepest; the question of finance, the ability and willingness of her country to supply her with a revenue—the possibility, however firmly signed and sealed the contract, that when the whole truth was out, obligations to an errant Queen who was also a Papist might be regarded as negligible. This was the only flaw in the pattern of Christina's future, but it was a very big one, and was capable of marring the whole. She made huge demands, probably on the principle that the more you ask the more you will eventually get. To begin with, following Whitelock's advice, she asked as her absolute property certain lands, including the port of Gothenburg. The suggestion was summarily refused. Only the revenue from the lands would be bestowed upon her, and Gothenburg was certainly too great a treasure to be sacrificed.

Finally she was granted the revenue from the fertile island of Öland, where Charles Gustavus had spent most of his days in a castle of beautiful stone like marble, which was quarried from the island itself and in great demand for fine buildings:[1] the island of Gottland, larger than Öland, but of less importance and little value: the islands of Ösel, Wollin and Usedom: the town and castle of Wolgast, and some lands in Pomerania were ceded to her, and the whole would bring in an income of two hundred thousand crowns.

In those days there might be seen great wagons rolling through the forest, skirting the lake with its four thousand

[1] Though Louis XIV would have none of it at Versailles. He found it *triste et mélancholique*.

islands—rolling along to Gothenburg, piled high with the treasures that Christina was taking out of the country. This activity had been going on so long and so secretly that few people realized the extent of it until it was too late to protest. Not only did she take the whole of her priceless library, and quantities of pictures and statues in marble and brass, the greater part of which she had collected herself, but she denuded the royal palaces of their finest furniture, gold and silver pieces of enormous value, and a vast quantity of jewellery and bijouterie which was the property of the Crown. In fact, she took away exactly what she wanted, without regard to anyone.

Marie Eleanore, meanwhile, had been in residence at Nyköping, and Christina had not altogether neglected her. Whitelock writes of her, wrapped up warm with furs, driving in her sledge over rivers and lakes and arms of the sea, to visit her mother, alas! as was often the case, in spite of Whitelock's remonstrances, on the Lord's Day. The last of these visits was made to announce her coming abdication. She took Charles Gustavus with her, and in the presence of the Court, told her mother that the time had come for them to part, and that in losing a daughter she was gaining a son. Charles was formally presented as that son, and Christina resolutely kissed her mother—a farewell salute—coldly and without a trace of emotion. Marie Eleanore, true to tradition, burst into tears, was led to her room and cried throughout the night. Again Christina was called to her bedside and attempted to console her. In the early hours of the morning she left Nyköping, and Marie Eleanore never saw her again.

One of Christina's last acts before she abandoned the throne was one of her most astonishing, because gratuitous. It showed the direction in which her mind was at the moment almost fanatically set. She sent a messenger by diligence to Stockholm, with a secret paper of which no one but she knew the contents. The messenger was to go to the Portuguese Resident, to open the paper and read it to him without letting him see it or handle it. The messenger found himself obliged to tell the amazed Resident that his employment at the Court was useless, because Christina had decided not to recognize the Duke of Braganza as King of Portugal, that title belonging to Philip IV of Spain and to him and his successors alone; that she had always considered Braganza as a usurper; that she thought it better to warn the Resident of this resolution so that he might have leisure to prepare for departure from a country in which he could no longer be received in a manner fitting to his position; that the Prince, her successor, would be in accord with her in this. Apart from her infatuation for Pimentelli, Spain was for the moment more important than any other nation, because Philip IV was interesting himself in her conversion, and because she was intending to spend some time in the Low Countries on her journey South. Her progress must be one long triumph, and everything should be concentrated on that.

The Senate was shocked when it heard of the insult to the harmless Portuguese Resident, but the conclusion was that it was Christina's way of getting the right side of Spain for her own purposes, purposes which were not quite clear to her Ministers, ignorant as they were of her ultimate intentions. The fact that this event happened only eight days before her abdication seemed to imply that as soon as Charles came to the throne relations could be re-established with Portugal, and the Minister, after lying low for a space, reinstalled. Meanwhile Christina would have achieved her object, and no one would be any the worse. Whether this was what Christina did mean or not, it was what happened, and by the time she was out of Sweden she did not mind what became of Portugal or its Resident.

Still the financial side of things kept her uneasy. It was fairly certain that Charles Gustavus would be punctual with his obligations—he could hardly do otherwise after all that she had done for him. But supposing he did not marry, and had no heirs and predeceased her? Anyone might come into power, and what was to prevent the repudiation of her claims? With no absolute property she was utterly dependent on the good faith of those at the head of Sweden, whoever they might be. Accidents must be guarded against.

A stipulation that she had made when she first made Charles Gustavus her heir was accepted by the Senate. It was that his brother Duke Adolphus, whom she disliked, should not inherit under any circumstances. Charles Gustavus might die young—he might be killed in battle. She decided that Count Tott must be nominated successor to Charles if he died without heirs. Tott had Vasa blood, being descended from Eric XIV, whose daughter married a Tott, and he was one of her most faithful friends. When Christina laid this proposal before the Senate, she was thanked for her solicitude for the throne, but was assured that since she had renounced it she renounced forever all authority in Sweden, either for herself or possible descendants. In other words she was not to dictate to them who should or should not succeed Charles Gustavus. Then she wanted to make Tott a duke, and to bestow a like honour upon Pierre Brahe, the First Senator, and the Chancellor Oxenstierna. All three declined and protested that their honour was satisfied in serving their country faithfully, without vain titles to hand down to their children, who should also be satisfied with the high places in their country's services they might be called upon to fill.

After this vain groping for a secure foothold, Christina was compelled to leave the future to Fate, and to hope that Charles would live to a ripe old age and do his duty by his generous cousin and benefactor.

Before her abdication the Senate asked her to withdraw the sentence of banishment she had passed on Magnus de la Gardie. It was pointed out that his offences so far as they knew did not merit such severe punishment. He was, after all, a Grand Officer of the Realm, and it would be a gracious act to pardon him before she laid down her crown.

"I have other things to think about," she said. "When I am gone the Prince can do as he likes, but please do not speak to me of de la Gardie again."

She refused to say good-bye to him, though she gave an audience of farewell to his wife. The result of this was that de la Gardie made a great noise about his delight at Christina's abdication, and declared that he would soon take office again. Charles Gustavus repudiated the possibility of reinstating one who had offended his benefactress. Nevertheless, Christina had not long been out of the kingdom before de la Gardie was back at Court and in high favour. This was not altogether surprising, since his wife was the King's sister.

For the great meeting of the Senate at which Christina was formally to abdicate, the stage was carefully set. The hall was hung with splendid arras, some of it from Whitelock's house; red cloth-covered forms were ranged for the senators, and at the upper end was the silver chair of state, with a rich cushion upon it, and a canopy of crimson velvet above it. First to enter were the Boors—members of the Council—about eighty of them, led by their Marshal. Then followed a hundred and twenty Citizens, led by their Marshal. All took their places and were covered. Then by the same door entered the Marshal of the Nobility, followed by about two hundred gentlemen of the first families. At their approach the Boors and Citizens rose and uncovered. Then came the Archbishop of Upsala with his Bishops and Clergy, while all the rest stood uncovered. When all were seated, the Queen's Guard entered, and many of her servants.

Lastly came the Queen, also with her head bare, and walked up the lane made by her attendants to her silver chair. Everyone except members of the Council then left the hall and the doors were closed.

Christina sat a moment in her chair, all eyes upon her, before she beckoned to the Chancellor. He came to her with respect, and after a short colloquy returned to his place. The Queen sat, pale and evidently deeply chagrined. Then she rose courageously and " advancing with a good grace and confidence ", says Whitelock, addressed the assembly in a speech that was entirely extempore. The Chancellor, whose duty it was to announce the cause of the Council being summoned, had, without warning her beforehand, refused point-blank to do it.

When, some days later, Whitelock alluded to this incident, the Chancellor explained that by reason of the oath he had taken to Gustavus Adolphus to keep the crown on his daughter's head, he desired to be excused from making the proposal. Whitelock remarked:

" Indeed, Her Majesty spake with an excellent grace and spirit, which was a wonder to see it done by a young lady to so great and grave an assembly; and the matter of her speech was pertinent and full of weight."

" Indeed," said the Chancellor, " she spake very well and materially, and like a prince."

After the Queen's excellent little speech, the Arch-bishop spoke at great length, begging her to desist from her intention of resigning the government, but at the same time extolling the virtues of the Prince, her heir. He was followed by the Marshal of Nobility and the Marshal of the Citizens, who both made long and flowery orations.

At last stepped out the Marshal of the Boors, " a plain country fellow, in his clouted shoon, and all other habits answerable, as all the rest of his company were accoutred. This boor, without any ceremony or *congés* at all, spake to Her Majesty, after this phrase:

" ' Oh, Lord God, Madam, what do you mean to do? It troubles us to hear you speak of forsaking those that love you so well as we do. Can you be better than you are? You are Queen of all these countries, and if you leave this large kingdom, where will you get such another? If you should do it (and I hope you won't for all this) both you and we shall have cause, when it is too late, to be sorry for it. Therefore my fellows and I pray you to think better on't, and to keep your crown on your head, then you will keep your own honour and our peace; but if you lay it down in my conscience you will endanger all. Continue in your gears, good Madam, and be the fore-horse as long as you live, and we will help you the best we can to bear your burden.

" ' Your father was an honest gentleman and a good King, and very stirring in the world; we obeyed him and loved him as long as he lived; and your are his own child and have governed us very well, and we love you with all our hearts; and the Prince is an honest gentleman, and when his time comes, we shall be ready to do our duty to him as we do to you; but as long as you live we are not willing to part with you, and therefore I pray, Madam, do not part with us.'

" When the boor had ended his speech he waddled up to the Queen without any ceremony, and taking her hand, shook it heartily and kissed it two or three times; then turning his back to her, he pulled out of his pocket a foul handkerchief and wiped the tears from his eyes, and in the same posture as he came up returned to his own place again."[1]

Christina's comment on this episode is interesting. When Whitelock remarked on how highly she was complimented by all the Marshals, especially by the Boor, she said:

" Were you so taken with his clownery? "

" It seemed to me as pure and clear natural eloquence, without any forced strain, as could be expressed."

" Indeed," said Christina, " there was little else but what was natural, and by a well-meaning man, who has understanding enough in his country way. . . . I think he spoke from his heart."

" I believe he did, and acted so, too, especially when he wiped his eyes."

" He showed his affection to me in that posture more than greater men did in their spheres."

It was like Christina to describe as clownery what had obviously moved her deeply. Till she was sure of Whitelock's attitude towards the incident she was not going to reveal her own sentiments. The episode of the clumsy boor with his filthy handkerchief and ridiculous tears must have made a diverting story for the Court snobs. Christina would have kept her emotion shut in her heart, not for the world to see. Here was indeed a single gem of value in a vast array of elaborately set imitations. Even Oxenstierna's devotion was more to the throne and the memory of Gustavus Adolphus than to herself. If he had had real affection for her, would he have risked a collapse in the abdication ceremony when, at the outset, he refused to play

[1] Whitelock.

the part which it was his duty to play? There was no reason why he should not have announced his conscientious scruples before the ceremony, and spared the Queen a situation which only her own wit and *savoir-faire* saved.

The next ceremony was the entry of Prince Charles Gustavus into Upsala. The Prince, in a pale grey suit, mounted upon a very brave grey horse, with pistols at his saddle and his sword by his side, waited for the Queen half a league outside the town. The whole Court and all the nobility and gentry in full panoply attended Christina, who " went gallantly mounted, habited in her usual fashion in grey stuff, her hat on her head, her pistols at her saddle bow ", says Whitelock, with twenty-four of her Guard in attendance.

When the royal cousins met they both dismounted. He kissed her hand, and stood bare-headed while she spoke to him, very respectful to her as his Queen. After a short parley, they mounted their horses again, and the procession to the town began, Christina turning often and calling to the Prince, who was riding respectfully in attendance on her—his Queen. Then he would ride beside her for a while, but always bare-headed.

So they came through great multitudes to Upsala, and to the Castle where the Prince was conducted to the royal apartments which Christina had given up to him. There was nothing left now but to resign the throne.

On the 6th of June Christina heard the Act of Abdication read in the Senate, Charles Gustavus by her side. She renounced the throne for ever for herself and her posterity, and recognized Charles as her successor, so long as he maintained her rights to her revenues. She promised on her side to do nothing that would injure the State. Another Act, in which the Prince undertook these conditions, was signed, after which Christina was clothed in her royal purple robes and the crown set on her head. Carrying the Sceptre and Ball, and preceded by two senators carrying the Sword and Keys, she entered the grand hall of the Castle and ascended the silver throne. On her left stood the Prince. Then the two Acts were read in a loud voice by Rosenhaue, and handed to each of the cousins. Now was the moment for Christina to deliver up the Royal Insignia. It was the duty of Count Brahe to take the crown from her head.

He refused.

This second unrehearsed incident was boldly faced by the Queen, who took it off with her own hands, and delivered the rest of the insignia to the Marshals. Then she threw off her royal mantle, which was subsequently torn into a thousand pieces by those present for souvenirs, and, in a simple garment of white taffeta, she stood and addressed the assembly in a beautifully delivered and moving speech, which few heard without tears. She then addressed the Prince, with many admonitions, among which was a request that he would not neglect Marie Eleanore, her mother.

The Prince made a pretty effort to lead her up to the throne again, and she smilingly returned the compliment, but he would not have it. Instead, he took her hand and led her back to her apartment, himself retiring to his own, which had so lately been hers.

The same afternoon Charles Gustavus walked in his ordinary habit through the thronged streets to the Cathedral, where he was crowned King of the Swedes, Goths and Vandals. After the ceremony, which was of the simplest, the whole city of Upsala rang with cries of "God save the King!" When the procession came to the court of the castle, Christina was seen at her window, with a cheerful countenance, watching the scene, and her deep voice was clearly heard as she wished her cousin joy of his crown and government. She did not appear again, and in the evening all the nobles feasted with " him who was the rising sun ".

Christina could not be persuaded to stay a moment longer in Upsala.

" How can you ask me to stay here where till now I have reigned as sovereign, and where I should see another with all the power in his hands? " came from her heart when Brahe begged her to wait.

There was still strong feeling among the people that she should stay and spend her revenues in Sweden, and it was because of this that she announced her departure for the Spa to take the waters. She fretted to get free from all entanglements, and she would not feel safe until she had crossed the border.

While Charles Gustavus and his nobles were still toasting and pledging, Christina stole away from Upsala in a downpour of rain.

PART II

CAP AND BELLS

CHAPTER VII

THE LABYRINTH

THE journey through Sweden was a dull anti-climax. Only sitting back in her coach that rainy night Christina could console herself with the nearly tangible sensation of all Europe stirring under the superb gesture she had made. But her departure was almost a flight, and so secret did she keep the details of it that even Charles Gustavus, King of Sweden, was deceived.

Imagining that she would go by sea from Kalmar to Germany, he ordered twelve ships of the line to be ready to escort her, but she sent a message at the last moment that owing to contrary winds she had decided to go by land and the Sound to Denmark. What did the commissioning of a battleship more or less matter to her, however exasperated the nation might be at more useless expenditure? So by land she went, and, disguised as the son of Count Dohna, who, with the faithful Steinbergh, was in attendance on her, she did most of the journey on horseback, her gun slung over her shoulder, a red scarf worn in the Spanish manner and her pistols at her side. Only four of her gentlemen attended her, and none of them had any idea where she was going. Clairet Poisonnet knew, for he had gone ahead as Marshal of her lodgings.

When she arrived at Helsingborg, the port for Denmark, an emissary from Charles Gustavus made a final but half-hearted appeal on his behalf that she would change her mind at last and marry him. He must have felt fairly secure on this point. Christina's reply was naturally a refusal. It was not likely she would care to return to Sweden as a mere consort after reigning as Queen. But it was quite a clever move of Charles's, and left an excellent impression, even on Christina herself, who was more than half taken in by it.

In spite of her disguise, the news of her arrival in Denmark spread like wildfire. Curiosity to see this famous figure drove the Queen of Denmark to disguise herself as a maid and wait on Christina at a country inn. This was Sophie Amalie of Brunswick, whose jealousy had driven Christina's friends, the Ulfelds, from the Danish Court. Christina talked of nothing but the iniquities of the Danish Queen all through the meal. Though she said when told of the identity of her waiting-maid: "What! that cabaret maid, the Queen of Denmark! Well, listeners never hear good of themselves. It serves her right," there is a strong suspicion that she knew of the plot beforehand, and rewarded the royal eavesdropper with much more than she bargained for. Probably Clairet was responsible for the whole affair.

The talk of Europe, though it was concerned with one burning topic, was a babel of diverse theories.

"Who is this lady who light-heartedly resigns what most of us fight and long for in vain?" cried Condé.

Christina had been anxious enough about his opinion to write to him before her abdication, hoping for the continuance of his admiration in spite of her change of state. She was sure to meet him at last in Flanders.

That her abdication was the act of a saint—that she had to renounce the throne because Sweden was getting too hot for her—that on the other hand her principal motive was to escape the horrible climate of her native land—that her aversion from marriage with her cousin which was being forced upon her drove her forth—that her vanity was not satisfied with the attention she attracted in Sweden—that she wanted to scandalize the world—that she was becoming a Papist because she wanted to be Queen of Rome—these were only a few of the theories propounded by the wise.

Christina was prepared for all this. She wrote to Chanut:

> I leave it to everyone to judge the affair according to his own lights. I don't know how I could withhold this liberty from anyone, and if I did, I shouldn't want to. I am not ignorant that some people will judge me favourably, and I am glad to think that you are one of that small number. As for the rest of the world they don't know my character nor my mood, as I have not explained myself to anyone but you and one great man among my friends [probably Pimentelli] as understanding as yourself.

When she had stood before the silver throne in her plain white silk garment, her royal robes and her crown gladly surrendered, she saw herself a free woman, a citizen of the world who by her own greatness would conquer men's minds and hearts. Her vast self-confidence would not even contemplate the possibility of any loss of prestige resulting from this voluntary resignation of her high estate.

She was Christina—unique and unassailable; and it was because she was Christina that, freed from the throne, she was going to be so much more astonishing a figure in history than she could ever have been as Queen of

Sweden, slave to her Parliament, her people and her throne. Her last State document was signed—her abdication, in which she discharged her people from the oath they had sworn to her.

" Christina, by the Grace of God, Queen of Sweden, of the Goths and Vandals, Princess of Finland, etc." Only four years ago the herald had cried:

" The most powerful Christina is crowned. Herself and no other! "

And now she stood stripped of her glory, bravely defying Fate. She, who had never been anything but Queen, had never known, had not even dimly visualized anything but absolute dominion, complete security. She did not see that, with the purple robe that slid to her feet and the crown she so firmly removed from her own head, went defences that never again could be summoned for her protection.

Heinsius, her honest philosopher, was profoundly right when he wrote to her:

" You have cast away your shield; of your flatterers few praised Christina, most the Queen."

Position is a surer guard than character; it is the only thing the world respects. Though Christina's morals had always been freely discussed throughout Europe, whatever criticism came to her ears only amused her. She knew she was invulnerable, and eagerly listened to the latest bit of gossip about herself; the more exaggerated it was, the more she was amused. But now the shield was gone; every shaft was going to hurt.

By the time she reached Hamburg the rumour of her conversion convulsed Sweden. The clergy demanded that her revenue should be reduced; indeed there was a strong movement that she should be deprived altogether for her breach and change of faith if the rumour were a true one. The fact that she was travelling *en cavalier* was also a vexation to her late subjects. Tales of her extravagant behaviour were already drifting into Sweden.

She had certainly thrown off her yoke with a vengeance. At Hamburg Pimentelli had arranged for her to lodge in the Jew Texiera's house, which was enough to scandalize the Lutherans. Christina was quite satisfied with her lodgings and host, and when she heard of the expostulations of the clergy from their pulpits, she remarked that after all Jesus Christ was a Jew and consorted with Jews all His life. She made Texiera her agent, and he played an important part in her subsequent battles over revenue.

At Hamburg she resumed feminine attire for a time, and there was no public sign of her conversion. She attended in state the church of St. Peter's, accompanied by the Landgrave of Hesse. Here a sermon was preached in her honour, comparing her to the Queen of Sheba. She presented the preacher with a gold chain; but his gratification was tempered by the discovery of a finely-bound Virgil in her pew, which she received with a smile when it was restored to her.

That was really rather a good joke.

She did not linger long in Hamburg. After a gorgeous entertainment in her honour "without the walls" given by the Landgrave of Hesse on July 30, which lasted until early morning, she set off, in male attire again, on her journey to Antwerp, accompanied by Steinbergh and her four other gentlemen, the rest of the retinue being ordered to meet her in Amsterdam later.

At Münster the Jesuit College was visited by a young gentleman of quality, who was shown and took a lively interest in the library, the church and the precincts generally. He chaffed the holy father on the morals of the Order, and its members being " all things to all men ". He heard Mass with his attendants, and after refusing the refreshment of a cup of wine, saying, " I am no wine-bibber ", departed, leaving everyone the better for his cheerful company. One of the Fathers, who had a portrait of Christina, saw through the black wig, big hat and high boots of her disguise, but he kept his own counsel until she was gone. Next day she sent a hundred ducats, which no doubt consoled the brotherhood for this feminine intrusion.

Holland was traversed incognita. She would not consent to a royal reception. She had little interest in that country, and only wished to get through this part of the journey as fast as possible. A girl she met on the road fell in love with her, and gave her a little amusement, but she was glad to get to Antwerp, where she became a woman again.

Here she lodged with a rich merchant, Gerard Salian, and her first visitor was the Archduke Leopold, who governed the Low Countries for Spain. She received him with great ceremony, going to the foot of the stairs to meet him, addressing him as Highness, and at the end of the audience conducting him again to the bottom of the stairs. They conversed in Italian. Because he represented Spain, Christina could not do him enough honour.

Condé was in Brussels, and naturally was as eager to meet Christina as she was to know him. The usual preliminaries were observed. Condé demanded the same ceremonial reception as the Archduke had had. Christina flatly refused to give it, knowing well how this attitude would please the Spaniards. Both were equally obstinate; it was a deadlock. But Condé's curiosity was not to be denied. He went to one of her receptions in the suite of a friend. Christina's keen eyes and instinct were not to be deceived. Apart from the obvious greatness of Condé, she had a nose for royal blood, and as soon as she saw him she approached him. He retired hastily but she pursued him. When she still followed him and came close, he muttered " All or nothing! " and escaped.

The situation was so very ridiculous between these two fine people, who should have known better, that their friends arranged a chance meeting where formality could be dispensed with. This took place when Christina was on a visit to Brussels. They met, and their disappointment with each other was not concealed. They walked up and down the Mall in the Brussels Park, talking very frankly and coldly. No one knows what they discussed, but whatever it was, they never discussed it or anything else again.

Another person who was curious to see, but not to meet, Christina, was Elizabeth of Bohemia, who travelled from the Hague for that purpose. She had not forgiven Christina for the death of Descartes, and she sat through an evening at the theatre, gloomily regarding the levity of her late rival in the royal box, and returned to the Hague but little consoled by the sight of her. Chanut also came from the Hague, bidden by Christina, who was anxious to see her old friend. This visit was at once construed as having political significance. It was at once assumed that Chanut was wanting Christina to intercede for peace between France and Spain. Chanut, horrified by this interpretation of a simple, friendly visit, wrote begging her to give the lie to the rumour publicly. She made matters worse by writing a violent letter of vituperation against France. Though Chanut's reply to this was a model of dignity and diplomacy, he thought it necessary to lay the whole correspondence before the Court of Sweden. King Charles Gustavus and his Ministers could only protest that they knew nothing about the matter, and understood less. It was evidently another of Christina's moves to flatter the

Spaniards, and as she was no longer in power in Sweden they were not responsible for her vagaries.

Christina stayed in Antwerp until December, combining a great deal of amusement with the serious business of her conversion. Her desire was to be received privately into the Catholic Church, and for the safety of her revenue, keep the matter secret, even though she should visit Rome. Innocent X was Pope at the time, and communication with the Vatican had for some time been established through Philip of Spain and Pimentelli, but there was not much hope that Rome would consent to keep so important a conversion secret. Meanwhile, rumour grew ever more insistent in Sweden, and there is little doubt that the rumour was a death-blow to the old Chancellor Oxenstierna, already sick and discouraged as he was. That Christina should cast aside the sacred trust of the crown left her by Gustavus Adolphus had been a bitter disillusion to the old man; but that she should forsake the faith that her father had so fanatically loved was almost sacrilege. He could not face this, and in August, only two months after her abdication, he died.

The journey from Antwerp to Brussels was made by canal, and at the head of the procession was the gorgeous State barge, gilded and richly decorated, in which sat Christina and the Archduke. The banks were lined with people and soldiers who fired volleys in her honour. The sun set on all this magnificence, and Christina, as she floated through the stillness, could see through the twilight the city of Brussels far away across the flat country, lit by bonfires and thousands of torches, shining each moment more brightly like a great star on the horizon. An elaborate illumined " set piece " over the gates, was discerned as they approached, with two angels holding up a laurel wreath crowned with the name of Christina. Cannon roared, rockets flared and all the bells of the city clanged and crashed as Christina went through the carpeted streets to the Archduke's palace, at three o'clock in the morning.

Later that day, Christmas Eve, in a private apartment of the Palace, she made her secret profession of the Catholic Faith.

Pimentelli was there, and so were Montecuculi and the Archduke. It was regarded as a miraculous coincidence that the artillery, which had had orders that all the guns of the city were to fire a volley at some time during the ceremony, hit upon the very moment when Christina was being absolved by the Dominican Père Guêmes who had been in attendance on Pimentelli in Sweden.

For seven weeks Christina was the guest of the Archduke. Her days and nights were filled with charming amusements. Mazarin sent a company of French players to entertain her. There were balls and hunting parties, tournaments and endless fireworks. Nor were the savants lacking. Vossius came to pay his respects, and was commissioned to buy more books, so he was able to add to his own library in the usual way. Gassendi, Bochart and Heinsius were among the faithful. But most of her protégés of the scholarly days became her bitterest enemies, and were responsible for much of the slander that was let loose in Europe, as soon as she abdicated, in lampoons and pasquinades, in striking contrast to the panegyrics of Stockholm.

Christina had wanted the Ulfelds to join her suite, but they had refused. There were other adventures in store for them. Ebba Sparre, too, had hurt Christina by declining to come with her. From Brussels she wrote to her:

> How supreme would be my good fortune if I could share it with you, and if you could see my happiness.

I assure you that the gods might envy me if I could only have the joy of seeing you. But as I cannot have this satisfaction, I can only pray you to believe that wherever I am in this world, I shall treasure your precious memory, and that over there, beyond the mountains, I shall carry with me the passion and tenderness I have always felt for you.

Keep me at least in your dear memory, and do not spoil by forgetfulness the happiness of the one being in all the world who honours you most.

Adieu, Belle.

Remember your CHRISTINA.

PS.—I forgot to tell you that I am perfectly well, and that I am the object of a thousand honours here, and on good terms with all the world, except the Prince de Condé, whom I only see at the play and the Court. My occupations are to eat well, sleep well, study a little, talk, laugh and see the French, Italian and Spanish comedies, and to pass the time agreeably. Lastly, I hear no more sermons; I distrust orators, and I agree with Solomon that all is vanity, and everyone should eat, drink and be merry.

. . . .

That miraculous volley of guns at the moment of her absolution had not only made a deep impression on the Faithful, but the occasion of it could not well be kept from the world in general. What happened in Brussels was immediately known in Sweden. There were spies everywhere, and it is not likely that so loudly proclaimed an event should not reverberate in Stockholm. The rumour of her conversion had now become a certainty, and another event put the possibility of any more secrecy out of the question. Innocent X, who had not definitely insisted on the immediate public proclamation, died, and was succeeded by Cardinal Fabio Chigi, as Alexander VII. The King of Spain had been trying to negotiate her secret reception in Rome, but when Alexander came into power he made it clear at once that she must openly avow her change of faith.

Christina again became seriously alarmed for her future. She knew the feeling that was growing in Sweden, and she could not ignore the reasonable resentment of her late Lutheran subjects at her duplicity. The Senate sent Count Tott to Brussels, hoping that his representations and the sight of one of the pleasantest people she had left behind her in Sweden might persuade her to change all her plans and come and spend the income they were going to be obliged to give her in her native land, and forget all about Rome and the Catholic religion. Few converts to Rome have escaped the futile eleventh-hour appeal from distracted relations and friends, and Christina was naturally less influenced than most by such a thing.

From Tott she gained a clear insight into the state of feeling in Sweden, and was driven to write an urgent letter to Charles X:

> Sir and Brother,—Count Steinbergh, who is returning to Your Majesty's side, will assure you by word of mouth of the goodwill that I feel towards your Person and the Crown. I shall always preserve these sentiments, and I should deem myself unworthy of life if I were capable of losing the love I have for my country, and the friendship I feel for Your Majesty. These are sentiments that will last longer than my life. And I beg you to believe that I should be happy to render some service to my country by which I could acquit myself of the obligations of my birth. Meanwhile, I

pray you to continue to give me your friendship, and to believe that I shall live and die,

Sir and Brother, etc.

CHRISTINA.

BRUSSELS,
March 30, 1655.

This letter was closely followed by another, more explicit, in which she frankly begs him to look after her interests, at the same time assuring him that she will never do anything that could prejudice the honour of the country she has left, and that all the evil rumours as to her conduct were false. She did not mention her conversion.

The progress of affairs with Rome went slowly, and Christina, after her visit to the Archduke, moved to the Palace of the Duc d'Egmont, where she began to live at her own expense. She had not been there long when all gaieties were suspended by the news of her mother's death in Stockholm. She retired to the country for three weeks, and when she returned to Brussels her life was much quieter, and the desire to move on towards Rome became keener. It was no use wasting money in Brussels which could be spent in Rome. There was nothing for it but to proclaim herself to the world and risk the consequences. The Pope was elated by the prospect of welcoming so distinguished a convert, and the advantages of her living in Rome were obvious.

Christina therefore started on her journey South in September. She had meanwhile collected her retinue, which was a very mixed assembly. The star was Don Antonio Pimentelli, who, as Ambassador Extraordinary to his Catholic Majesty Philip IV, was attended by a suite of twenty persons. Don Antonio de la Cueva y Silva was Grand Equerry, and his wife, of Flemish birth, chief lady-in-waiting. Their suite consisted of eighteen persons. A good many odd people attached themselves in various capacities, in order to travel at Christina's expense to whatever destination on the road suited them. There were only four Swedes in the whole company, which amounted to about two hundred souls, including a guard of twenty-five, the Dominican Father Guêmes, only five women, and, of course, Italian musicians who were an absolute necessity to the Queen wherever she was.

France was gracefully represented by, among others, Gabriel Gilbert, the Parisian, her secretary. He was the author of plays good enough for Molière and Racine to dip into and help themselves when at a loss for *quelques bons mots*, and plenty of ingenious light verse, from which the following quatrain will serve to speed Christina and her cheerful company on their way:

A LA REINE DE SUÈDE APRÈS SON ABDICATION

En servant cette Reine égale aux Amazones
Je n'aurai pas perdu six ans:
Car qui sçait donner des couronnes
Sçait bien faire d'autres presens.

CHAPTER VIII

THE ROAD TO ROME

Charles Gustavus had not only sent Count Tott to Brussels, but he had given him letters addressed to numerous kings and princes for Christina to present as she passed through their domains. In this he showed that he was not confident of her reception in her altered circumstances. It was a decent but tactless action, and Christina spurned these letters of introduction. Her own glory and fame were passports to the whole world, even, surely she was convinced, to heaven itself when the time came. Montecuculi was sent on ahead with a letter to the Archduke of Innsbrück announcing her intention of staying in that town on her way to Rome.

There was little incident on the journey from Brussels, except a visit from King Charles II of England and the Duke of Gloucester at Königstein. Christina was one of the many ladies Charles had wanted to marry. Whitelock had been shocked to hear herself confirm the rumour of his proposals, but until this moment she had not seen the exiled King. It was observed that when they conversed he uncovered, and remained so throughout the interview, " with great reverence ". They talked for two hours.

Through historic Nördlingen she went, and would not stay for banquets offered her, but pressed on, through Frankfurt, Rottenburg, over the Danube to Augsburg.

Here she was shown a table at which her father had dined after one of his victories. She shed a few tears for the memory of the great Gustavus Adolphus. But the Alps were in sight, and every day the call of the South became more insistent.

On the 26th of October the ascent of the mountains began, and at Zirla, a little village, she was met in state by the Archduke and Archduchess who conducted her to Innsbrück. Here Monsignor Holstenius had everything prepared for the public reception of Christina into the Church. With him had come Père Malines, who had been one of the disguised visitors to the Court of Stockholm. He was sent to meet the Queen, and explain to her the details of the ceremony as desired by the Pope, and she expressed herself ready to obey the orders of His Holiness with great humility.

On the 3rd of November Innsbrück was *en fête* for one of the most remarkable ceremonies it had ever seen. Christina, clad in a severe black silk gown with no ornament save a wonderful cross composed of five large diamonds, walked through the carpeted streets to the Cathedral, where she renounced the faith of her fathers. She read her long profession in a clear, deep, emotional voice, kneeling, with the Archduke and Pimentelli beside her, and at the end a Jesuit preached a sermon on the text: "Hearken, O daughter, and incline thine ear; forget also thine own people and thy father's house."

Great rejoicings followed this ceremony, and in the evening an Italian musical comedy was played before the Queen. This was considered inappropriate to the solemn occasion, and a sort of apology was offered to Christina for the want of taste of the organizer of the entertainment. Christina, who had thoroughly enjoyed it, replied:

"Gentlemen, it is most appropriate that you should

entertain me with a comedy after the farce I played for you this morning."

This remark, so typical of Christina, was seized upon by her enemies and indignantly repudiated by her admirers. No doubt the atmosphere, in spite of the Italian comedy, was hanging rather heavily about her, and it was her pleasure to lighten it. She enjoyed a pageant while it lasted and her profession was sincere, but now that it was over her spirits began to bubble over again. She could not be serious for long, and her reactions were swift, her temperament resilient.

Next day she wrote this letter to Charles Gustavus:

> SIR AND BROTHER,—I have arrived here safely, and I have received the permission and orders of His Holiness to declare myself what I have long been. It is a great happiness to me to obey him; and I prefer the glory of obeying him to ruling over the dominions which are now yours. You should be pleased with this resolution of mine, even though you disapprove of it, because it is so much to your advantage. I assure you that it does not alter my affection for you, nor the love I have for Sweden, which will never change.
>
> Your affectionate sister and friend,
>
> CHRISTINA.
>
> *November*, 1655.

While the four replicas of her profession were being made, the days were spent in "virtuous recreations", according to her historian Gualdo. The documents were signed by Christina; one she kept herself, one was sent to the Pope, and the other two were placed in the archives of Innsbrück and the Vatican.

And now at last—Italy!

Perhaps the journey from Innsbrück to Rome was the happiest and least troubled period of Christina's life. There was all the joy of anticipation; there was the glorious satisfaction of being the most discussed figure in Europe—a crescendo of gossip was almost audible even as she crossed the Alps. What would the errant Queen do next? Anything was possible. The world was watching for new developments. And a soothing fact was the momentary absence of financial cares. A handsome present from Charles Gustavus towards the expenses of her journey and a huge loan effected in Antwerp solved all present problems. On the 8th of November the company set out, escorted for a few miles by the Archduke and all the nobles of Innsbrück. Over the Brenner pass to Stenzing; over the clear Adige river to Trent, where the Prince of Trent entertained her with great pomp. The Venetian Republic, having no wish to waste money on useless entertainments, and being engaged on its fifth war against the infidel Turk, had forbidden her and her company to enter the State of Venice, on the pretext of plague in the country they had passed through. They contented themselves with a present of fish, plenty of compliments and good wishes for her journey.

Then across the river Po to Rovere, where the Duke and Duchess of Mantua came to greet her; and here, it is sad to relate, she was also greeted by rain, which fell with tropical violence for two days. In spite of the mud, the usual ceremoney of descending from their coaches for a formal greeting was observed, the Duke standing bareheaded, and both parties entreating one another to get in out of the rain and mud.

A gorgeous banquet was held in Christina's honour at the Ducal Palace, from which Pimentelli was absent on account of ill-health, and then in pouring rain she set out across the fens for Ferrara. Half-way there she was met by the four nuncios sent from Rome with a Papal brief for her, and a special carriage and travelling-bed to bring her to Rome. Though she had renounced for the moment travelling *en cavalier* and went in her coach and six English black horses, she was dressed on this occasion in a black velvet cape of masculine cut, with wide collar and grey trimmings.

But what pleased her more than the Papal brief or the travelling-bed was the sight of the Marchese Girolamo Rossetti's wonderful bridge over the Po at Ponte del Largo. It was wide enough for four carriages to pass abreast, rested on forty-six great *barcone*, and was one of the most beautiful constructions in Europe. A luxurious barge decorated with the arms of the Pope and Christina had been prepared to take her across the river at this point, but she insisted upon going by the bridge, which was immediately lined with soldiery not only to salute the royal party, but to demonstrate the solidity of the structure.

Two days *festa* for Ferrara! Christina was now in the Papal State, and she sent Montecuculi to Rome with letters of humble thanks to the Pope for his graciousness. Don Luigi Pio di Savoia, brother of one of the nuncios, gave a great banquet for her at Ferrara. Music and painting were discussed. Music, she said, was the ornament of princes, and her favourite artists were Bernini and Pietro di Cortona. On the subject of architecture she declared that St. Peter's in Rome, the Duomo in Milan, and St. Paul's in London were surely the greatest cathedrals, but the latter had, alas, become a stable.

Another glass of wine!

Never had she drunk so much wine as since she came into Italy, but then, never had it tasted so good.

At this there was some respectful drollery. Cardinal

Vescovo ventured that in his opinion she drank nothing but water. Two glasses of wine were nothing but *due sorsi.*

A really amusing banquet, and her first intimate encounter with members of the Sacred College.

Everywhere the same ceremonies greeted Christina. Salvos, fanfares, triumphal arches and fireworks—banquets and special Masses in all the churches. In deference to the great learning of the royal traveller, academies were organized for her amusement, long panegyrics were read by the leading local intellectual lights, and many ladies, no doubt radiant stars in their own ambient, were moved to recite poems in her honour. At Bologna there was a magnificent tournament by the principal nobles and gentlemen of the city in which more than a hundred and fifty lances were broken. This kind of entertainment Christina preferred to second-rate academies. At Faenza specially elaborate preparations had been made for a display of local talent. No fewer than thirty compositions, ecclesiastical and secular, in several languages, were to be recited as spiritual food for Her Majesty after the usual banquet. But no sooner was the banquet finished than Christina rose hurriedly, announcing that she was obliged to continue the journey immediately, though it was late in the evening and no preparations had been made. She had most decidedly not come to Italy to be bored. Whatever her taste may have been in human beings, in intellectual matters she was fastidious.

At Forli she had to endure an academy, but was consoled by the present of a wonderful white horse which she had admired. She set off in full panoply again, astride her horse, and was met by the Governor of Rimini, and it was twilight when the cavalcade entered the Piazza, which was gaily illuminated, and at the doors of the Palazzo Pubblico nobly dressed pages held torches as she passed. On the stairs she found a large company of ladies quaintly attired, who performed solemn and well-rehearsed dances for her before the inevitable academy began.

The next important place was Pesaro, and to Christina it was more important than she guessed. A great company came out to meet her, including the very eminent Cardinal Homodei, Legate of Urbino, with fifty of his Swiss Guards. But more notable even than Cardinal Homodei were two young gentlemen of what Gualdo calls *nobiltà conspicua,* the Counts Francesco and Ludovico Santinelli, sons of Count Alfonso Santinelli, the first knight of Pesaro.

This fascinating pair of brothers, if not conspicuous for their nobility, were conspicuous in the entertainments arranged for Christina. They first attracted her attention at the *festa* held in her apartments on the night of her arrival. They opened with a *gagliarda*, and because they were dancing with capes and swords, Christina begged them to remove both, so that she could see them better. They then danced another *gagliarda*, which so delighted Christina that she called for a *canario*. They executed this with delightful grace. Francesco Maria counted among his many accomplishments the making of verse, and Christina had already been presented with a finely bound volume of his poems, consisting chiefly of praise of herself. After the dancing she supped privately to the music of a violin and lute.

Next day, after hearing Mass in the monastery of St. Catherine, and spending some time with the nuns who were famous for their singing, she lunched publicly with the Cardinal. Here Francesco Santinelli had the honour of serving her. After lunch the Queen was again enchanted by the Santinelli dancing. This time it was a Spanish *Cachuca* and Ludovico the agile performer. The academy which followed was naturally more sophisticated and amusing than those of the less important cities, the more so as the talents of the Santinellis were again in evidence; for Francesco was responsible for the whole programme, which Christina later declared to be the most diverting entertainment of all her travels. She cannot be blamed for falling a little bit in love with the Santinellis.

At the next point in her journey, Sinigaglia, a ridiculous *comedietta* was performed by the brothers, which had been written by Francesco in a single night for her amusement.

And this was not the end of the tale of their accomplishments. After the *comedietta* she was curious to see how these two young men sat a horse. There followed a splendid exhibition of horsemanship and swordsmanship before which all her defences fell, and they were, with very few formalities, attached to her suite as gentlemen of the chamber, which is no doubt what they had been playing for.

At Loreto, as soon as Christina saw the cupola of the sanctuary in the distance, she descended from her horse and knelt reverently. Later, she laid at the feet of Our Lady of Loreto a beautiful sceptre and crown set with diamonds and pearls, on one of which the face of the Virgin was clearly visible. This was obviously a symbolical act of homage, but next day when she was asked if she would like to see where the precious objects had been put, she said:

" No, such bagatelles aren't worth looking at."

The gesture was done and finished with.

The rest of the journey was a crescendo of fireworks, rejoicings, rain, mud, and sometimes snow. At Storta, a few miles out of Rome, two cardinals of royal blood headed a great procession that came out to greet her in the name of the Pope. One of the cardinals was Frederick of Hesse, whom Christina had tried to dissuade from joining the

Church a few years ago. Though her entrance into Rome was strictly incognito, she was accompanied by an imposing company of cardinals, noblemen, coaches and cavaliers and Pope's Guard. She rode in a state coach and wore her usual grey dress, black cape and no jewellery but a single ring. Rome was reached late in the evening. In spite of the hour a huge crowd waited in the Vatican gardens, and had no compunction in following her into the Vatican itself.

"Is this how one enters Rome incognito?" she asked, laughing.

But the Pope was waiting for her, and soon she was walking between two cardinals through the vast torch-lit galleries of the Vatican, eager to see the only being on earth whom she considered worthy of her homage.

With her hands crossed on her breast she knelt at his feet. For the first time in her life she humbled herself—a new sensation, and for that not to be despised. The Pope, as enthusiastic as she at the meeting and all it implied, raised her and set her beside him under his canopy, a place of honour conceded to few. Thus they conversed for half an hour. This interview, and all subsequent private audiences, were conducted with open doors; Alexander was not going to risk a repetition of the scandal regarding the sainted Gregory VII and Mathilda of Tuscany.

Courtesy seemed to demand that Christina should be invited to spend at least her first night at the Vatican, as her arrival was so untimely and the weather so unpleasant. Fortunately there were the apartments built by Innocent VIII, so far away from His Holiness's own quarters that there was no fear of the slightest embarrassment. Alexander himself had supervised the preparation of the Queen's retreat, which looked upon the magnificent Belvedere gardens. With exquisite sensibility he ordered an inscription under the figure of Tramontano (North wind) to be erased from the Torre de' Venti, for fear she or her people should take it amiss. It was "*Omne malum ab aquilone*".

Christina was guest at the Vatican for a few days, and the first morning she was up at an early hour—she must have had no more than her usual allowance of three hours' sleep in spite of the physical and mental strain of yesterday. She wandered in the Belvedere gardens with Montecuculi and Monsignore Acarigi, Cup-bearer to His Holiness, conversing in French, and no doubt admiring with interest the incomparable statuary therein. The Rhodian Laocoon had pride of place in those gardens, and in niches to protect them from the weather were many of the glorious statues which are now to be seen only in museums. Fountains were playing and perhaps the sun was shining while Christina walked in the Belvedere gardens with her companions. The "bel vedere" was of Rome, and her short-sighted eyes gazed out with wonder at the city of her desire.

The silver coach, litter and sedan chair designed for her state entry into Rome by Cavaliere Bernini—where could they be seen?

Her curiosity was immediately satisfied. Bernini was sent for. He was probably only just round the corner superintending the great work of his life, St. Peter's Colonnade. He was at any rate at hand, and took Christina to see the Pope's gifts, which were wonderfully designed with elaborate figures and many inventions of the great sculptor. Sky blue velvet and silver galloon were used for the hangings and upholstery, and for the six pure white Neapolitan horses that were to draw the coach there were draperies of the same and silver harness. Christina examined every detail with enthusiasm.

"Whatever is bad about it is my work," said Bernini with affected modesty.

" Then none of it can be yours," she declared.

Now she must see the white saddle-horse the Pope was also giving her. The beautiful animal was led out, and Christina mounted it at once. She proceeded to give a remarkable display of horsemanship, performing some feats bareback to the amazement of the onlookers. A yearly tribute from Naples to the Pope was a *chinea*—a pure white horse, probably a small breed with an Arab strain, and it was one of these that Christina was finding so responsive, so quick to turn, so lively and mettlesome.

Silver coaches were all very well—anyone could ride in them. . . .

The Vatican library was then explored, and Holstenius, who was librarian, must have shown her treasures she envied, most of all two parchment Virgils of a thousand years ago. Holstenius himself had a collection of rareties, one of the finest in Europe. So Christina's first day in Rome was after her own heart. Her public entry into the city was supposed to take place three days after her arrival, but the preparations were so vast that it had to be postponed. Instead, His Holiness visited Christina in her apartments, and they walked up and down conversing (with curtains and doors wide) in her private room. When he left her, it was observed that she accompanied him to his chair and shut the door of it with her own hands, with many other pretty acts of reverence.

The day of the State entry was a Roman holiday. Bombs and guns resounded from daybreak. But again the weather threatened to spoil everything. In a deluge Christina set out from the courtyard of the Belvedere in the Pope's carriage with her huge following, through the Porta Angelica and outside the gates to the villa built by Giulio III, and there for several hours the vast company waited for the rain to stop. Just when it had been decided to abandon the procession the clouds broke, the sun burst through, everybody cheered up and the great cavalcade started. At the Porta Flaminia, now the Porta del Popolo, the immense procession was met by the College of Cardinals on horseback, and here Cardinal Barberini welcomed her in the name of the community. The gate had been completed by Bernini in her honour after Michael Angelo's original design, to which had been added an inscription commemorating the "happy and joyous entry of Queen Christina" (*Felici faustoque ingressi Christinæ Suecorum Reginæ*) A.D. 1655. Over the gate the Papal arms, six hills surmounted by a star, were united with the Vasa sheaf of corn, which was not unlike the fascia of modern Italy.

Bernini's silver coach and litter were notable features of the procession, but they were empty. At the last moment Christina had decided to enter Rome on her white *chinea*. Bernini's own sentiments on the occasion are not recorded, but Rome was amazed to see the regal convert astride her steed, booted and spurred, as though for the chase instead of her solemn reception into the Catholic fold.

Alexander had impressed upon his cardinals and those about the Vatican that this Queen from the North was not likely to understand Latin ways. Decorum must be strictly observed. No chattering or spitting. Let them beware; the honour of the Church depended greatly upon their behaviour. The steps of St. Peter were lined with cardinals when Christina dismounted in the Piazza and strode up the steps to be received by them. She wore a mantle of black over her grey and gold *just-au-corps*, grey and gold breeches (some say white) and a huge cavalier's hat heavily plumed.

Whatever the cardinals may have thought about decorum, whatever they may have expected to see, they did not flinch, not even the ancient Gian Carlo and Sforza, who by reason of their years and position were detailed to lead her to the Pope who stood at the High Altar. Here she was received, and the Piazza of St. Peter resounded with the deafening explosions of bombs great and small, while she kissed the toe of His Holiness, and he declared that her conversion was so precious that heaven itself must be *en fête*.

Two days later, on Christmas Day, she was confirmed, taking the name of Maria Alexander, the latter in deference to the Pope and because Alexander the Great was one of her heroes. Her last day at the Vatican was signalized by an invitation to dine with His Holiness. As the rule forbade his eating at the same board as a woman, they had separate tables, the Pope's being a few inches higher than hers. Likewise his chair of red velvet was slightly more exalted. But she had a royal seat specially made for her, surmounted by a canopy. Don Antonio de la Cueva, her Grand Equerry, and Francesco Santinelli were in attendance on her. Conversation was not necessary, because a sermon was preached by the Jesuit Father Oliva throughout the lengthy repast, during which Christina interpolated a few observations which everyone found brilliant and to the point, but which were not recorded. After dinner they were again in private conversation, and the evening concluded in Christina's apartments with a musical and dramatic entertainment.

Next day, with many regrets expressed on both sides, Christina exchanged the hospitality of the Vatican for Palazzo Farnese.

Life in Rome had begun at last.

CHAPTER IX

PALAZZO FARNESE

PALAZZO FARNESE of the Dukes of Parma, which is now the French Embassy, was designed by Sangallo for Alexander Farnese who became Pope Paul III in 1534. It was finished by Michael Angelo for Cardinal Alexander Farnese, grandson of Pope Paul, and is supposed to be built partly of stone from the Colosseum, which was at one time used as a quarry by all and sundry architects. History enough in the classic structure itself to stir the imagination of the Northern Queen. But within the splendid frame, with its square and terraced court, its three orders of columns, and its roof garden, were priceless examples of painting and sculpture beyond even Christina's dreams.

The Toro Farnese was still there; it was not moved to Naples until 1786. Caracci had done his greatest work in the upper gallery, covering the walls and ceilings with marvellous painting in deep relief; Salviati and Zuccaro had decorated the great hall. Christina, no doubt, knew the fame of every detail in this treasure-palace before she entered it. She must have heard of the altar service of deeply cut crystal which was unique—chalice, bell, sprinkler and crucifix all of purest crystal wrought with the holy story; and of the marble head supposed to be a portrait from life of Christ.

There was no room for her own enormous collection

of treasures, most of which, with her library, was still at Antwerp. When she took possession of the Palazzo after her visit to the Vatican, she was amused to find many of the world-famed statues swathed in white draperies. Even Venus looked coyly over her shoulder from a muddle of chaste folds. Christina had them all removed at once, and hung a number of her most lascivious masterpieces without delay.

"How like a priest!" she said when told that "Monsignore Governatore" was responsible for this error of judgment. A bewildering person, this virgin queen with her odd collection of courtiers and ideas.

The salon she longed for materialized. Princes, cardinals, and all the leading figures in art and politics flocked to the Farnese. The great Roman families vied with each other in entertainments of unheard-of lavishness. Prince Pamphili, who had cast away his cardinal's hat to marry the beautiful Olimpia Aldobrandini, Princess of Rossano, built an enormous amphitheatre outside the Pamphili Palace, to accommodate Christina and the aristocracy of Rome while they watched horse-racing and masquerades; with fêtes, suppers and the like it was estimated to have cost them forty thousand crowns. Not to be outdone, the Barberini and Palestrini put up an amphitheatre to hold six thousand persons, where not only comedies and operas were performed, but elephants and various wild animals appeared, fountains played and all sorts of artful natural phenomena took place.

Christina thoroughly enjoyed these spectacles, but the aristocracy of Rome were soon made to understand that she took no interest in themselves. The ladies complained very soon of her haughty manner, and her insistence on such etiquette when they visited her that they were all kept standing for hours till they fainted, whereas rumour said that when only men were present, everything was apparently as easy as could be. The ladies of Rome were so indignant that they began absenting themselves from her salon, which was exactly what Christina wanted. She had no time for Court ladies unless they had special gifts. . . .

> How happy I should be if I could see you, Belle, but I am condemned by Fate to love and appreciate you always without ever seeing you; and the jealousy of the stars towards human felicity prevents me from being entirely happy, because I cannot be that, separated from you. Do not doubt this, and believe me that wherever I am in this world, there will be somebody who is entirely yours, as I have always been. But is it possible, dear Belle, that you still remember me? Am I still as dear to you as I was in the old days? Didn't I deceive myself when I imagined that I was the person you loved best in the world? Ah, if that is so, do not undeceive me; leave me my illusion, and do not grudge me the happiness of thinking myself beloved by the most charming creature in the world . . . believe that, no matter what happens, I shall never cease to be yours. Adieu Belle. A thousand kisses.
>
> CHRISTINA ALEXANDRA.

This was to Ebba Sparre a fortnight after her arrival in Rome. She never ceased to desire the company of her favourite maid-of-honour, and was constantly sending letters and messages—not exactly begging her to come, but making it very evident that she was wanted. In five years Ebba was dead. How long, if she had lived, Christina would have gone on loving and wanting her it is not easy to surmise, but she was certainly the only woman who inspired a lasting affection.

No, she had no time for Court ladies, and she certainly

had no time for the strict etiquette observed by the Roman aristocracy. She renounced the throne to escape from these things, though her insistence on certain occasions on small points with regard to her own dignity grew more marked as she realized how much she had surrendered with her crown.

Pimentelli seems to have already lost ground with Christina before Rome was reached. De la Cueva was head of the household, but now the majority in power were Italians, and the most important of these was Francesco Santinelli, who was now Grand Chamberlain.

Now Fate led the Marquis Monaldesco to the Farnese with a recommendation from Cardinal Mazarin.

Santinelli and Monaldesco! If Christina had searched the world she could not have found a more perfect pair of blackguards. Ludovico Santinelli was nearly as generously endowed with fascinating qualities as his brother, but he seems to have had, if not a conscience, at least a sense of what was the limit. Or was it only envy of Francesco's superior gifts that made him cry "*Voilà qui commence bien!*" when he found him selling Christina's plate and jewellery and pocketing the profits himself?

Santinelli and Monaldesco soon found each other out. The obvious course was to form an alliance, and under their leadership the servants robbed and pillaged undisturbed. Gold and silver galloon was torn from the furniture. Priceless pieces of silver—cups and chandeliers particularly—were removed and plated copper substituted. Pimentelli's coach was ravaged even while he waited on the Queen. Splendid doors were torn down and used for firewood. It was as though a herd of wild beasts had been let loose in the Farnese. The Marquis Giandemaria, whom the Duke of Parma had deputed to do the honours of the Palazzo, was in despair. He appealed to the Pope, to Christina herself, who blamed de la Cueva for not attending to his duties. Things came to such a pass that when the Queen and her attendants visited the Fulvius Orsinus museum which was housed in the Palazzo, Giandemaria was reluctantly obliged to have the company followed and watched throughout their peregrination.

Christina was perfectly indifferent to the behaviour of her people. She submitted to being robbed and cheated, chiefly because, acutely conscious that their salaries were badly in arrears, she found it more expedient to shut one eye, even though the depredations were not confined to her own property. Responsibility was the one thing she was determined to avoid, and she flung herself into her new-born freedom with a zest only tempered by the usual misgivings as to ways and means. In spite of her insane extravagance which was enough to make the most imprudent gasp, she could not ignore the instability of her financial affairs. The huge sum borrowed in Antwerp had vanished, and the Swedish revenues had not yet made their appearance.

Scarcely had Christina abandoned her throne when Charles Gustavus led his people to war against Poland. The Swedish government was delighted to be at the old game again, and every crown that could be raised was poured out on it. Christina was apprehensive of the future. Supposing her country should repudiate its obligations on the score of her conversion or the necessities of the campaign against Poland? Where would she be? What on earth could she do? She could not hope that Alexander VII would make himself responsible for her vast expenses, though he had made her a generous gift on her arrival. This was only a *gentilezza* which could not often be repeated. There was no hope but Sweden, and Sweden had made no sign.

Such were the anxieties that gnawed at Christina's consciousness while she sat at the play or entertained Rome in the Caracci gallery or gazed at the new comet, or discoursed at the academy she founded, which was to be known for centuries as the Arcadia. Must freedom always be tempered with preoccupations even in the short hours she allowed herself for sleep? The present was all very well. Debts and promises, usurers, and pawnbrokers carried one along on a huge wave of extravagance, but on what sort of a beach was one going to be stranded? Something definite would have to be done about it if freedom was to be enjoyed at all. Her secretary, Appelmann, one of the few Swedes in her suite, was sent to Sweden to make a proposal to Charles Gustavus. It was that he should give her a lump sum of a million and a half crowns for all the domains assigned to her for revenue. She knew that there was little hope of getting this from a country that was already impoverished by her own recklessness, and she proposed as an alternative to exchange the Swedish domains for Polish domains as yet in the process of being conquered. Even this uncertainty, she considered, was better than what she foresaw would be an endless struggle for her rights. If all this failed, Appelmann must suggest selling or mortgaging some of the lands apportioned to her. Finally, as a last resource, she demanded the right for herself and her Court to practise their religion without interference if, as was probable, she was obliged to come herself to Sweden to look after her interests.

Appelmann's mission was not altogether unfruitful, although he failed to secure any of the new privileges she demanded. Charles Gustavus advised her to leave things as they were, because any alterations would involve long delays. Though he did not want her in Sweden, his disposition towards her was always generous, and the delays and difficulties were due, not to his own want of consideration, but to the continued reluctance of the Senate to disburse on her account. Christina was soothed soon after Appelmann's return by remittances that temporarily eased her situation. But she was promised an income of ninety-four thousand crowns, which should have kept her in comfort and dignity if she or her advisers had had the slightest idea of the value of money.

The ecstatically cordial relations between Christina and the Pope were doomed to wither almost at flowering. A blight had threatened even while the Queen was on her way to Rome, when discreet inquiries at the bank of Santo Spirito instituted by His Holiness revealed the fact that as yet there was not a *paolo* deposited to her credit. This might mean nothing, and his doubts were quenched in the surge of pride at the world-wide sensation his distinguished convert was creating, for by now he had persuaded himself that he was responsible for her conversion. He had been prepared to receive a devout lady full of fervour and good works, who would as like as not spend her days in conventual seclusion, distributing largesse among the Papal charities with an eager hand, and contributing in every possible way to the glory of the Church. But what was the use of a royal convert who made not the slightest show of piety in public?

"Better an Ave Maria before the world than a thousand prayers in private," he insisted, presenting her with a rosary which she declined to use.

"*Non mica voglio essere Cattolica da bacchettone,*" she said.

Far from consenting to make a show of praying in public, she behaved in St. Peter's much as in the old days at Stockholm, only instead of playing with dogs she chatted with cardinals. Then there was that uncomfortable incident of Cardinal Colonna, who was over fifty and should have known better. He fell in love with Christina, and even went to the undignified length of serenading her at night. The Pope ordered him to leave Rome at once, and further scandal in that quarter was averted. But the scandals of her household increased daily, and Alexander was kept fully informed. He soon saw that his misgivings over the Santo Spirito inquiries were well founded. Christina had nothing to give, and indeed it looked as though she might become dependent on the Vatican—so wildly uncertain did her future appear, so wrapped in boreal fog the materialization of her phantom revenues. Now that he knew her better, no doubt he regretted his weakness in the matter of books on the Index. She had asked his permission to read all the forbidden books. He granted this as he would have granted anything in the first rapture of her conversion, but even then he made an exception of the Old Testament and one other book. As for the Old Testament, she must have studied that long ago in the same curious spirit in which she read Plato and Tacitus.

It was impossible with an entourage of such mixed nationalities to steer clear for long of jealousies and factions. The Spaniards, led first by Pimentelli, had been so long predominant that they were not likely to endure any rivals. But Pimentelli, now that he had helped to achieve the intervention of Philip IV in Christina's approach to the Pope, had served his purpose, and in the matter of personal charm he had long been superseded by Santinelli. De la Cueva began to resent Santinelli, who was loaded with favours, and even sat beside Christina when she drove in her coach, which privilege had so far only been enjoyed by de la Cueva as head of her household. While this slight was rankling, M. de Lionne from the French Court was received by Christina in exasperatingly long audiences. De la Cueva at last expostulated. France was the enemy of Spain, and here was a portrait of Louis XIV in the Queen's chamber, obviously brought there by de Lionne. What did it mean?

It meant, said Christina, that she was not a subject of the King of Spain, and that if she chose to be friends with France it was nothing new, for she had always been that, and in short she was not going to be dictated to by Spain or anyone else.

De la Cueva in a rage left the Farnese with his lady and went to the Spanish Embassy. Christina did not want this, and tried to lure him back with a present of seven horses. But horses did not appeal to Don Antonio. He went about Rome slandering the Queen, declaring among other things that she was *la maggior putana del mondo*. Pimentelli joined him fervently in the campaign against Christina's character, and the chief factory of slander was from this time the house of Cardinal de' Medici, where the Spanish faction used to meet.

However wide the breach between Christina and her late Grand Equerry, etiquette demanded that he and his lady should take their *congé*. All the principal members of the household were assembled for this occasion, and after de la Cueva had kissed her hand and asked her pardon if he had not served her as well as he should, Christina replied in ringing tones that his conscience would tell him if he had served her well, and that if she ever heard that he had spoken disrespectfully of her again she would see that he got his deserts, wherever he might be.

"As for you, Madame," she said, turning to the wife, "I thank you for having followed me from Brussels and for your services. If you have been chattering about me, I cannot blame you, because you are only a woman."

On this she dismissed them both, and said afterwards

if he had not been a general to the King of Spain she would have had him bastinadoed. De la Cueva and Pimentelli both left Rome, and the Italians had it all their own way at Palazzo Farnese. The war between French and Spanish was only an echo in Christina's suite. There were the French and Spanish factions at the Vatican. Cardinals d'Este and Barberini led the French faction and Cardinal de' Medici the Spanish. Between these two groups was the "flying squadron" (*l'escadron volant*), which was composed of the intelligentsia who resented foreign influence at the Vatican, but were ready to take advantage of either side for the benefit of the Church. Cardinal Homodei, Cardinal Imperiali, and the French Cardinal de Retz were brilliant members of this group. The leader was the youngest of them all—Decio Azzolino.

Through the haze of Santinellis, Monaldesco and their like, this star, that was to shine throughout Christina's life with a steady fire, had not yet penetrated. Her sympathies had been with the flying squadron from the first, and much of her time had been spent in colloquy with its leaders, chiefly with Borromeo, Barberini and Azzolino. She had had plenty of opportunities of appraising Azzolino's admirable intellect. She was immediately impressed by the young cardinal, with his finely tuned Latin mind active and deft as a swallow, with his wit and remarkable good looks. He was constantly at the Farnese, expounding the policy of his party, and discussing poetry and the arts and all the subjects that delighted Christina.

Then there were notes sent to and fro—so frequently that there was quite a flutter in the Vatican about them, and Azzolino was obliged to give a written declaration that his relations with the Queen of Sweden were entirely innocent. Azzolino's birthplace was Fermo, an archiepiscopal see in the Marches. He belonged to the *petite*

CARDINAL AZZOLINO

noblesse, and began his ecclesiastical career at a very early age. He went to Spain as secretary to the Nuncio Pancirola, who made him his conclavist when Urban VIII died and Innocent X was created Pope. This led to his being established as Secretary of State, and being entrusted by the Pope with many duties in which his high qualities of mind and scholarly gifts were invaluable. Then the Pope, after the marriage of his nephew, Prince Pamphili, to the beautiful Princess of Rossano, adopted a certain Cardinal Astalli, and it was thanks to this prelate's underhand dealings with Spain and freeness with Vatican secrets that Azzolino owed his early promotion. The Pope promised a cardinal's hat to whoever should discover the means by which Astalli still communicated with the Spanish Ambassador after he had been forbidden to do so. Azzolino, who slept in the Montecavallo Palace, spied on Astalli and found that after the Pope had gone to bed he crept out by a little winding stair at the bottom of which was a gate leading to a narrow street, through which he walked disguised to a hackney coach that took him to the Spanish Ambassador's, where he stayed for two or three hours. When the Pope heard this he had him seized, deprived of all his honours, and sent him to Sicily as Bishop of Catania, where he shortly afterwards expired of grief.

That was how Azzolino, at the age of thirty-one, became a cardinal. But whatever happened, his early and rapid success was certain, because he had every possible gift for it, and any amount of ambition as well. And he was man of the world enough not to be too scrupulous when it came to the point.

Christina was too much engrossed with her Grand Chamberlain to take more than an intellectual interest in the most striking figure of the Sacred College at the time. Besides, she was already stretching out for something new.

Rome and its intrigues had become boring. The de la Cueva incident had poisoned the air. Something new and unpleasant had appeared in her life.

Mingling with the people in the street at some fête she would be elbowed—a mask thrust into her face would whisper an insulting word and be lost in the crowd. Direct and horrible contact with reality! This she had never known before. To be regaled with stories about herself from the security of the throne was amusing enough. It could not seriously touch her. Now here was the first unmistakable indication that it was not going to be so easy to keep her majesty intact, and at the same time live the untrammelled life she had promised herself.

That whispered insult was like a sting on the cheek. The memory of it, and others like it, set her heart beating with apprehension. Her nerves were on edge. She became ill in April with serious gastric disturbances. The doctors said she had eaten too much fruit, but it was more than that. *Dispiacere* had outweighed pleasure in this first visit to Rome. She needed a change. A visit to Louis XIV and his mother was indicated. The French Academy was ready, she knew, to give her the welcome her gifts and erudition merited. She was longing to see the Grande Mademoiselle whose career she envied. And then perhaps on to England—Whitelock had practically invited her—to be the guest of Cromwell, whom she admired so much.

But it was difficult to contrive a good excuse for leaving Rome so soon, after only four months, and with all her financial affairs in such a muddle. Why not pretend to arrange a journey to Sweden via France to settle up her money difficulties? No objection could be raised to that. Her projected departure was announced. Cardinal Mazarin was advised that she wished to pass through France, but without any ceremony. This last request was designed to make the story plausible. Only a greeting to the royal family and the Cardinal as she hurried through on her urgent journey to the North. But the Pope was seriously alarmed. Did this incontinent desire to leave Rome mean that her enthusiasm was already on the wane, and that she was going back to her Lutheran Faith? Christina had become, in these few months, more and more of a puzzle to him. She seemed entirely devoid of piety, sometimes almost light-headed, yet the vigour and fineness of her intellect, the great qualities of heart that she sometimes revealed, convinced him that here was a personality that might become a saint—that might become one of the finest ornaments of the Church, if only managed with discretion and tact. He had not discovered the way to deal with her before she startled him with this disconcerting project, which might mean anything.

If only Christina had had patience, she need not have created these doubts in the mind of Alexander, and could have saved herself the annoyance of dissembling, for the outbreak of plague in Naples roused a scare in Rome which gave a perfectly valid excuse for flight. Having now this excuse ready to hand, she lacked the means for the journey. Nearly all her jewellery was pledged either to her own advantage or Santinelli's; the Swedish money had evaporated; the coffers of the Farnese were empty. Her diamonds followed the rest of her jewellery and brought in twelve thousand crowns—a wretched sum. There was nothing for it but to appeal to the Pope. She began by asking him for a loan of his galleys to carry her to Marseilles. After a good deal of hesitation he consented to this, but when she asked for a loan of money, he did more than hesitate. He argued with himself that to lend her money, even with the promise of its all being paid back, would not be decorous.

If, as was more than possible, there was no restitution of the loan, he would have lost the money, and be merely counted as one of her creditors. If, on the other hand, he made a gift of the sum she asked, he would be no worse off than if he had " lent " it, financially, and the world would ring with tales of his generosity. Obviously, if it was to be ceded at all, it should be a handsome gift. He even went so far as to have special medals struck in silver and gold, on the reverse of which was represented the Porta Flaminia with its new inscription and Christina walking between the two cardinals. This should serve as a reminder to her of the glory of that great day of her reception, in case she should be tempted from the fold. These medals were presented to her in a purse, to which was added the sum of ten thousand crowns, with an apology for the poverty of the gift. Christina wept with emotion for the generosity of His Holiness, and preparations for the journey were put in train at once.

Monaldesco was now Grand Equerry in place of de la Cueva; Francesco Santinelli was still Grand Chamberlain; a suite of sixty persons consisting almost entirely of Italians was to accompany her. Only three women were in attendance, and they were rather simple *femmes de chambre* than ladies-in-waiting.

In June Christina left Rome on her new adventure. She went on horseback to Civita Vecchia, " the Pope's Town ", accompanied by several cardinals, and she and her suite embarked on four of the Pope's galleys for Marseilles.

Christina was often in tears on this voyage, and she was constantly gazing at a portrait which she carried about with her.

It was the face of Cardinal Azzolino that she was regarding with so fixed and passionate an interest.

CHAPTER X

PARIS AND COMPIÈGNE

At Marseilles Christina was welcomed in the name of Louis XIV by his Grand Chamberlain, the Duc de Guise. Her request for no ceremony was as little regarded as no doubt she had meant it to be. Louis XIV had ordered that she was to be received with all the pomp and circumstances due to a reigning monarch. But ceremonies did not prevent the journey to Fontainebleau from being a diverting adventure for the traveller and her escort. M. le Duc was enchanted by the Amazon ways of the Queen and her spirited conversation. He presented her with three of his own perukes, one of which she always wore under a huge plumed hat that she took off and on as she did her little cavalry cap at Stockholm. She was good fun, he found, and magnificent company for a man whose experience of women was so wide that novelty was hard to come by.

There was a piquant little episode at Lyons which might have been a bit of play-acting for his amusement. M. le Duc was evidently taken with her boyish ways. That pretty lady at Lyons was certainly her type, but probably if the Duke had not been there she would not have been embarrassed by such a violent assault on her beauty. Christina "*la baisait partout; la gorge, les yeux, le front, très amoureusement et mesme la voulait baiser la langue à la bouche, et coucher avec elle, ce que le femme ne voulut pas.*"[1]

At Fontainebleau Christina was met by La Grande Mademoiselle, heroine of the Fronde, who was prepared, after the tales she had heard of the Swedish Queen, to laugh at her odd ways and mode of dressing. But quaint though she might be with her crooked little figure, her short petticoats and cavalier's hat, and her boy's boots, Mademoiselle found, to her surprise, that she did not want to laugh, but was impressed by the beauty of the flaming azure eyes and the general air of " a pretty little boy " that she presented. But she could not approve of the Queen's behaviour at the play: " In her praise of places that pleased her, she would swear by God, throw herself back in her chair, tossing her legs about and assuming postures hardly decent." She talked agreeably on many subjects, and sometimes fell into a profound reverie, sighing deeply and coming to herself suddenly as though waking from a dream. They went to see some firing on the water at night. Christina held Mademoiselle's hand, and when the latter winced at a near shot she cried: " What! a young lady who has seen so much and done so many fine things, afraid? " She then confided to Mademoiselle that the desire of her life was to be present at a battle. This desire, in spite of all her efforts, was never to be gratified.

The Court was at Compiègne at this time, and after a few days at Fontainebleau, Christina set out again and made a state entry into Paris, on a white horse and clothed in scarlet. Her welcome from the people of Paris was all that royalty could desire. Patin says that such a crowd had never been seen. Wherever she went her public appearances were always successful. She had a magnetic charm which she could exert to the destruction of all

[1] Edouard Palatine of Bavaria.

criticism, and her sense of the stage never failed her. Sometimes she could not resist making grimaces at the crowd, and a favourite trick was to make a lightning change of clothes in her coach—queen to cavalier and vice versa. She knew when to be gracious and sweet, and her magnificent outbursts of obscenity were often prompted by the desire to stir up things when they were becoming monotonous. This was the case when, before her departure from the Louvre in Paris where she was lodged, she astonished a large and distinguished company which had been basking in her graciousness, with a resounding oath of such grossness that even the Duc de Guise, who was present, turned pale.

The motive underlying her keen friendship with France was, under the circumstances, surprising. It was inspired by nothing less than the desire for another crown. Emancipation had already revealed its drawbacks, and, after all, a throne ensured some certainty as to revenue. One was, at any rate, not a poor relation grudgingly provided for. The fantastic project upon which she was bent was the conquest of the kingdom of Naples. Herself at the head of an army of French troops would wrest the crown from her late friend and protector, Philip of Spain. There were already French troops in Italy serving under the Duke of Modena, who was friendly to France and the scheme. Monaldesco was to be Field-Marshal. That ill-starred favourite was busily engaged in secret negotiations already. Funds for the enterprise must be conjured from somewhere, and Christina, already an adept at devising ways and means, conceived the idea of mulcting France of at least part of the large debt she still owed to Sweden on the Thirty Years' War subsidies. Mazarin would, of course, be against such a scheme, but the pill would be well wrapped up in the promise that she would make a Prince of France her heir, and the prospect of putting another spoke in the wheel of Philip of Spain. She must have discussed this project with the Duc de Guise as they travelled from Marseilles, for he had governed Naples for a while with immense success until the Spaniards imprisoned him and seized the kingdom once more. Five kings of different nations had reigned in Naples within two years. It was a kingdom worth conquering. Five hundred leagues in circuit, it consisted of twelve large provinces, with twenty archbishoprics, over a hundred bishoprics, thirty castles and plenty of princes, dukes and marquises. Best of all, the King's revenue was at least three million crowns a year.

A fair land and a sweet and lovely climate, fit for a queen.

At Chantilly Christina rested, and it was here that Mazarin first met her. They dined together, and afterwards a great crowd of people came to pay their respects. Among them were two young men who attracted her special attention. When they knelt to kiss her robe she raised each and kissed him on the cheek. Mazarin presented them as young gentlemen of quality.

" I can well believe you. They look to me worthy to wear a crown."

She had recognized Louis and his brother, for Louis, says St. Simon, was as easily distinguished as a queen bee in her hive. For a youthful lark they had ridden over from Compiègne to get a private view of the Amazon Queen before the formal ceremonies on the morrow. Louis was a shy, diffident lad in those days, but it was noticed how eagerly he conversed with Christina as soon as she had, by calling him *mon frère*, revealed that his identity was no secret to her. She found him enchanting; she liked his grace of bearing, his grave and sweet countenance, and most of all his radiant youth. He was shyly in love, she knew, but deeply, with Olympe Mancini. Christina made friends with him and held him long in conversation. After this delightful interview Louis and Philippe galloped back to Compiègne in the dark. Next day the new château of Maréchal de la Motte-Houdencourt, a few miles out of Compiègne, was the scene of Christina's formal meeting with the King and Anne of Austria. Standing on the great terrace in front of the house, the Queen-Mother and her two sons, surrounded by the Court, in habits of gold and silver embroideries and all very gay, waited for the arrival of the interesting guest.

A flourish of trumpets and she appeared, not this time on horseback but driving with the Duc de Guise and Cardinal Mazarin. As soon as she saw the Queen-Mother she descended from the carriage. Though Anne had been prepared for an unusual-looking personage, she was amazed at the appearance of Christina, and afterwards declared that she had never imagined anything like her. It was certainly not one of Christina's best days in the matter of costume. Her semi-masculine coat was carelessly put on, showing more than was necessary of her crooked shoulder. Her peruke was awry and dishevelled, and there was some lack of cohesion between her shirt and collar. Nothing met when it should, with the result that expanses of back and neck were unnecessarily revealed. Perhaps the drive had been dusty, for her face looked ill-washed, and as for her beautiful hands, they were filthy. The first impression she made on this delicately *soigné* Court was more of fear than pleasure. In spite of this she was annoyed by the eagerness of the exquisite mob which surged into the house after her and surrounded the two Queens so closely that they were obliged to escape from it into the house, Christina keeping well ahead to make it quite clear that she was taking precedence with

Anne. There was a great deal of talk about this at the time, and some said that Louis later on reproved his mother for giving way to her. But it would seem a natural courtesy to the guest whose anomalous position as queen without a throne called for privileges rather than rights.

There followed a gorgeous feast. Christina ate with appetite, and anyone listening for pearls of wisdom was disappointed in her conversation, which was light and negligible.

Over there was Olympe Mancini.[1] The Duc de Guise pointed her out. She was staring, like everyone else, at the fascinating guest. Christina half rose in her chair and saluted the dark charmer. Later on she amused herself by encouraging the affair with Louis, making herself his confidante and assuring him that if she were in his place she would marry where she loved. Her influence was strong enough to cause his mother some anxiety. Whatever she might think of Cardinal Mazarin, she had no wish for his niece as a daughter-in-law. The Cardinal himself was against it, because, as Christina says, he knew that marriage was a sovereign remedy for love and the nuptial bed its tomb.

Christina wrote to Azzolino of Louis:

> He talks little but well, concealing his feelings with marvellous address, so well that I am of the opinion that they are never very violent, and in consequence he has not much difficulty in controlling them. He is more civil and courteous than it is possible to imagine. I think he will be valiant, and indeed that he is already, and will certainly be a great

[1] Not to be confused with Maria Mancini her sister, with whom Louis XIV fell more seriously in love later on.

prince if he ever takes his duties seriously. At the present moment he is absorbed in fine clothes, horses, hunting and dancing, and is a marvellously good athlete. He is tall, well-made and handsome, but less so than he is painted. Finally he is in love with the Mancini, but with such moderation and virtue that I don't believe that in all the three years he has been paying attention to her he has ever dared to touch the tip of her finger.

The first evening at Compiègne Christina was taken to see the Italian Comedy. It was very bad, and she did not hesitate to say so. Generally, she was assured, the comedians did better.

"I should hope so," she replied coldly. "Otherwise you would not keep them."

Apparently there were no women in attendance on her at this moment, which may account for her unkempt appearance that day. At any rate, Madame de Motteville says that her toilet that night was superintended by some of the King's *valets de chambre*, because she was without attendants. "She had neither ladies, officers, equipage, nor money," says this diarist, who was always inclined to exaggerate. But Christina had not the least objection to being waited on by men on the most intimate occasions. They were in and out of her apartments as a matter of course, and they did not fuss her as a herd of women attendants would, with their ridiculous ideas about inky fingers and clean linen. However, the King's valets seem to have accomplished something, for she appeared next day with her peruke curled and powdered, her face improved by a night's repose and some fresh spring water, her hands clean and a flame-coloured *just-au-corps* above her grey skirt.

A good performance by the Comédie Française Company compensated for the Italian fiasco, and Christina was loud in her praise, even while the play was going on. A tragedy acted by the Jesuits, however, on the 18th September was a sad affair, and Christina laughed rudely at it. There were fêtes of all kinds during her short stay at Compiègne, but affairs were not neglected and the Naples project was discussed at length with Mazarin, who was not going to commit France to anything definite, and soothed Christina with the promise that, if she could get the Pope's approval, something might be done. With this she had to be content, and set off from Compiègne, leaving mostly pleasant impressions behind her, though there were some who said she only left just in time.

At Senlis she visited Ninon de Lenclos. Ninon says in a letter to Madame de Sevigné that they talked of love, but Christina does not mention the subject of their conversation, which was long and engrossing. The journey to Italy was broken at Savoy, where she was received in great state by the Duke and his Court, but the *Duchesse Mère* complicated things by insisting upon taking precedence of Christina if they met. This suggestion was, of course, repudiated by Christina, and a deadlock was only avoided by her retiring to bed and pretending to be ill, so that the Duchess could visit her in bed and no one's dignity would be any the worse.

At Turin, having got into communication again with the Duke of Modena about the Naples project, she decided to send Monaldesco back to Paris to try and get something definite out of Mazarin. The plague was still raging in Rome, so from Turin she set off for Pesaro with the idea of visiting Venice. But Venice again was unwilling, and this time the war with the Turks was given as the pretext for postponing her visit. This was enough to make Venice the most desirable place in the world, and there is a story that she went there dressed as a sailor. She made her headquarters at Pesaro, and was in constant correspondence with Azzolino. It was grievous to have to postpone seeing him again. He was already trying to help her with counsels of economy, with little success. When he begged her to reduce her guard, which was ever increasing, Santinelli exclaimed:

"Better to be without bread than without guards!"

Christina was quite ready to agree with him. One could not have too many men about, and Santinelli was busy enrolling the youth of Pesaro and Bologna. He was still Grand Chamberlain and in high favour. Two women joined the suite about this time, with their husbands, Count Rangoni and Vicino Orsini. Donna Barbara Rangoni was fifty, had hair "more dead than alive" and one black tooth in the middle of the rest. She could never have been good-looking, but was gallant and proud. She had wit, dressed in the French manner, and was ambitious. Madame Orsini was a few years older, made up heavily, had no teeth at all, and went to confession several times a week. These portraits are drawn by Monsignor Lascaris, who was Azzolino's representative and kept the Cardinal minutely informed of all that went on. In one letter he writes:

> Her Majesty is more beautiful and *dévote* than ever. Yesterday she put on a gown of black velvet, trimmed with many blue ribbons and a very fine man's collar. It was enough to drive one mad, most of all when, picking up a certain French comedy, she began to read it aloud by the light of a candle. She read the rôle of Diana in love with Endymion so well that several times I was on the point of saying to her:

"Madame, though I am called *lasca*, I declare that in truth *cefalo* would be a better name."

Santinelli followed Monaldesco to Paris, as the Naples negotiations seemed to be hanging fire. He returned with fifteen thousand crowns, and a message from Mazarin that, though favourable to the scheme, he would rather postpone it to a more propitious moment. That was the best Santinelli could do, and of course the sum was quite useless for any serious purpose. Christina was discouraged, and her thoughts turned towards Rome. Santinelli was dispatched at once to find out if the Farnese was still at her disposition. No sooner had Santinelli departed than all plans were changed. She would go to France again; this Naples project must not be dropped entirely, and if she were not on the spot Mazarin would never come to the point. All through the summer letters were going back and forth between Paris and Pesaro, and every letter of Mazarin's was more discouraging. He stressed the importance of getting the Pope's interest, and the risk to the cause of her coming so soon again to France. Santinelli came back from Rome full of the great reception she would have if she returned, and with optimistic assurances as to the expenses of the journey and re-establishment at the Farnese. But Christina had quite made up her mind. She was going to France whether Mazarin wanted her or not.

It must have been during this hot and rather trying summer that the differences between Santinelli and Monaldesco began to develop. The wonder was that they had managed to keep friends for so long, for each had good cause to be jealous of the other with regard to Christina's favour—so evenly was her affection balanced between the two. Both were ambitious and unscrupulous.

It was a question only of which was the cleverer, and Monaldesco was soon to demonstrate that one can be too clever.

The ladies Rangoni and Orsini proved too much for Christina; their wit and piety were not enough to compensate for their dental failings. In their places Christina engaged the sisters Portia, Ottavia and Francesca Passaglia Giustiniani, handsome girls who, despite their impressive name, were simple *femmes de chambre*. Two of them, Portia and Ottavia, faithfully served her till her death. Francesca died young, but Portia and Ottavia married Italian gentlemen and became ladies-in-waiting.

Now the first act of the Monaldesco drama begins. Santinelli was not to come to France. He was sent back to Rome with six thousand of the crowns from France to put the Farnese in order for her occupation later on. With two thousand two hundred he was to reclaim the Queen's diamonds which had been pawned to pay for her first journey to France. He did reclaim them, but only to pawn them again with a Jew for his own advantage. He spent nothing on the Farnese, in which he had really only been able to get a small apartment for himself. He charged to the Queen's account the expenses of a gentleman-in-waiting whom he declared was necessary to his rank and position. This gentleman did not exist. So sure was he that out of the vast disorder of Christina's affairs no villainy, however blatant, would ever be discovered, that he coolly helped himself to her gold and silver plates, selling some, and altering the coat of arms to his own on others. He even went to the length of burning embroideries to extract the gold and silver from them. It was all so easy that he scarcely took the trouble to conceal his thefts from the world, with the result that someone sent the news to Monaldesco.

Christina started on her new journey in July, and her first halt of any importance was at Lyons. Here the historian, Galeazzo Gualdo, joined her suite and became one of her most fervent supporters. She was full of affairs, and sent the lesser Santinelli, Ludovico, with a long letter to the Duke of Modena, setting out her plan of campaign. By this time she had managed to get a definite invitation to the Court of France, but was begged to stay at Fontainebleau till the King returned to Paris from Compiègne. At Fontainebleau she arrived in October, and began again attempting to adjust her revenue complications. Appelmann was sent to Sweden to try and negotiate new proposals which in the end came to nothing. Meanwhile, Ludovico Santinelli had come back post haste from the Duke of Modena, and Christina amused herself by ordering from des Touschelles the equipment of her entourage for her entry into Naples. There were forty violet liveries for the Swiss Guards, embroidered with crimson and white passement, violet livery for two dozen pages, for twenty-five footmen, three coachmen and twenty-four *palefreniers*. Clairet Poisonnet was to be clothed in grey trimmed with gold galloon and black velvet. The *femmes de chambre* all had complete new wardrobes, and the Queen herself six new *just-au-corps* of different colours and material, each with a sword, a baudrier, and " a pair of men's boots for riding ".

CHAPTER XI

THE COAT OF MAIL

WHILE Christina was scheming for her revenue and designing her liveries, her mind was preoccupied with the certainty that in her most intimate circle a traitor was to be found. Letters signed by Francesco Santinelli had come into her hands. A French lady-in-waiting is supposed to have shown them to her, but it was always Christina's habit to examine the correspondence of her suite, especially when she had some secret project on hand. The contents of these letters were never divulged, but if written by Santinelli they were damning evidence against him. However, there were other things going on for which Santinelli could not be responsible, as he was in Rome. After much probing of the matter, she sent for Monaldesco, and revealed her doubts.

"Madame," he said, "you are betrayed, and the traitor is either someone absent that you know well, or myself. It must be one or the other. Your Majesty will soon know who it is, and I beg you not to spare the culprit."

"What does a man deserve who betrays me in this way?"

"Your Majesty should execute him without mercy and at once. I offer myself to be either the executioner or the victim, because it is an act of justice."

"Good. Remember those words of yours, and believe me, I shall not pardon him."

Those were bold words of Monaldesco's, and he must have been foolishly confident in the security of his plot against Santinelli. But as the days went by and vastly important letters that he was expecting failed to reach him, he began to get uneasy. If his correspondence went astray it would be a serious thing—a very serious thing. It was necessary to find another method of communication more reliable. He set about this with great caution. But not enough; Christina knew that this was the time to strike. She had all these important letters of Monaldesco's in her keeping; his villainy was clearly proved.

On the 6th of November she sent for Père Lebel, Prior of the Mathurins of Fontainebleau. She received him in the Galerie des Cerfs.

"You wear a habit that encourages me to speak to you confidentially. Promise me under the seal of the Confessional that you will keep this secret that I am going to tell you."

"In these matters I am blind and dumb," he assured her.

She put a packet into his hands. It was heavily sealed and without address.

"Mark well the day, hour and place of my giving you this, and return it when I ask for it in the presence of whom I choose."

The mystified priest retired with the packet and put it in a safe place.

On the 10th of November Monaldesco was ordered to go to the Queen in the Galerie des Cerfs. She was in the habit of giving audiences there, and there was nothing unusual in the command. Yet the Marquis delayed, and, when he did appear, it was easy to see that he was greatly disturbed. He was pale and agitated, and his agitation was not lessened by the sight of Ludovico Santinelli and two others who stood beside the Queen, their hands upon their swords. She held him in ordinary conversation for a few minutes, but she had sent for the Prior, who was on his way with the packet. No sooner had he entered than the door was securely shut behind him. The Queen called him to her.

"*Mon père*," she said, "pray give me the packet which I put in your care, that I may read it."

Taking the packet, she contemplated it for a moment, then, opening it, she took out some letters and papers.

"Do you recognize these?" she said to Monaldesco in ringing tones.

"Madame," said Monaldesco, trembling, "those are nothing but letters in your own handwriting!"

"But what are these?" She produced from the packet the originals of the copies, crying, "Traitor! Explain these if you can."

At first Monaldesco tried to inculpate other people, but finally, realizing how much she knew, he threw himself at her feet begging for pardon. As he did so, Ludovico Santinelli and his officers drew their swords. Frantic with apprehension, Monaldesco seized Christina and drew her into one corner of the gallery—then into another—all the time entreating her to hear his justification. She conceded this, and listened with patience to his feverish explanations. Then, leaning upon her ebony cane, she turned to the Prior and said:

"*Mon père*, I ask you to bear witness that I have not been hasty, but have given this villain more time than he deserves to justify himself—if it were possible."

She then ordered Monaldesco to surrender all the papers he carried about him. Among them were letters forged in Santinelli's hand (which was not unlike his own), one addressed to himself, and also the original drafts of these letters in his own handwriting. No one knows what was in them, but it was enough for Christina. She told the priest to prepare him for death and care for his soul; at which he joined in the supplications for Monaldesco.

"Why should I have mercy? This traitor is as bad as any criminal sent to the wheel; I have confided in him my most secret thoughts and my most important affairs, as to a faithful subject. I won't reproach him with all the favours I have showered upon him as though he were a brother; his own conscience should be his executioner."

With this she went from the gallery to a room adjoining.

Monaldesco threw himself at the feet of the Prior, asking him to plead with the Queen again for mercy. Santinelli and his officers surrounded him with drawn swords, telling him to confess quickly. His hour was near. His cries for mercy were so heartrending that Santinelli was moved to go himself to Christina and beg her to spare his life. But he came back and with tears in his eyes, said:

"Make your peace with God. You must die."

Again there was a dreadful scene. The Marquis, beside himself with fear, implored the Prior to plead again with the Queen. Christina was still coldly determined, and all the tears and supplications of the priest could not move her. Then he ventured to point out that as she was the guest of the King, she should consider very carefully before she insisted upon the execution taking place. To which she replied that she was not lodged by the King as a fugitive or prisoner, that she was her own mistress, and that she was answerable to God alone for her actions. Besides, there was precedent for this act.

"Yes, queens have done such things before, but it has been in their own realms."

The Prior went on to say how hurtful it might be to the honour and reputation she had gained in France—

perhaps he said enough to persuade her that it might be hurtful also to her political schemes. At the end of the interview she showed signs that if she had dared she would have revoked the order. But it was too late now. Monaldesco at liberty after this would be an unthinkable danger. There was no way out.

Lebel returned to the gallery, and taking the poor wretch in his arms, told him to resign himself to death and to make his confession. Monaldesco gave a piercing shriek and flung himself at the feet of the Prior and began his confession. While it was going on the door at the end of the gallery opened and the Queen's Almoner appeared. Here was a friend who perhaps could save him, and without waiting for absolution Monaldesco hastened to the new arrival and begged him to intercede with the Queen. They stood for a while in whispered conversation, and then the Almoner went to the Queen accompanied by Santinelli.

Santinelli came back alone, and said firmly:

"Marquis, make your peace with God, for you must die without delay. Have you confessed?"

He pressed him with drawn sword to the end of the gallery under the picture of St. Germain. Monaldesco's misgivings of the last few days had led him to don for his protection a heavy breast-plate of mail; this only served to prolong the dreadful agonies of his death. He was wounded in the stomach, and trying to draw his own sword to parry this, three fingers were cut off his right hand. Then Santinelli, having been impeded by the coat of mail, attacked his face. At this he cried:

"*Mon père!*"

The Prior came to him, and on his knees he made his confession, the blood pouring down his face, begging forgiveness for his crime, pardoning his executioners, and praying that he might meet death bravely. He then fell to the ground, and Santinelli attacked his head with such violence that flesh and bone were scattered on the pavement. At this the victim turned and lay on his face, making a sign that they should put him out of his pain with a thrust at his neck. Two or three thrusts had little effect, for the coat of mail was attached to his collar, and a mortal wound was impossible. While this was going on, the Prior was exhorting him to resignation and patience, which was probably as irritating to the executioners as it was useless to the victim. Santinelli suddenly turned to the priest, exasperated and nerve-racked.

"How is this to be ended? Cannot you help?"

The priest, indignant, replied that he could not advise. He was for the life, not the death of Monaldesco.

"Forgive me, *mon père*. I was wrong to make such a demand."

Then the Almoner appeared again at the other end of the gallery. Monaldesco, who had lain waiting for the last thrust, seeing his friend, rose, and with his last strength, dragged himself along the wall towards him. With clasped hands he spoke in a low voice and the Almoner made the sign of absolution, standing on the left of Monaldesco, beside Santinelli. No sooner had he left the gallery than Santinelli cut the throat of the Marquis, who fell, never to speak again. But he lived for another quarter of an hour. Lebel said the De Profundis, and when life was extinct Santinelli turned over the body and searched the pockets. There was nothing left in these but a book of the Hours of the Virgin and a small knife.

Santinelli and his companions went to announce the consummation of the dreadful deed to the Queen. Monaldesco had been summoned at one o'clock, and died at a quarter to four, so Christina had waited nearly three hours in that anteroom while the torture was going on.

But she was calm when they told her, and said that she deeply regretted having had to execute the Marquis, but justice must be done to traitors. Lebel was commanded to remove the body at once, and because it was heavy and the way was rough and night falling, he had it carried on a hand-cart to the church of Avon near Fontainebleau. The Queen sent two footmen with a sum of money for Masses for the soul of the Marquis, and two days later he was buried with all the ceremony and devotion possible. On his tomb was simply:

CI-GÎT MONALDESCO

No doubt, waiting there in the chamber so near to the Galerie des Cerfs that fatal afternoon, Christina was appalled by the fiasco which was being made of the execution. One swift thrust through the heart, and the traitor dead at Santinelli's feet—that was what she had visualized. Who could have foreseen the coat of mail that turned what she considered an act of justice into a prolonged and bloody torture? As the messengers came to her, each time more agitated, more urgent, she must have suffered.

The affair was being bungled; too much blood was being spilt—the pavement of Les Cerfs was drenched—and when Santinelli came to her flushed, distraught and exhausted by the ghastly scene that would not end, and then the Almoner with the tale of horror that he could scarcely tell, she was driven at last to cry:

"Cut his throat! Tell Santinelli to cut his throat!"

As he stood by Santinelli after giving the absolution, the Almoner must have whispered that message from the Queen, so swiftly did Ludovico give the finishing stroke that should have been given long ago. The dexterity of the swordsman had probably been hampered from the first by subconscious misgivings as to the legality and decency of the act, and a possibility of the Queen's changing her mind too late. It is not likely that Ludovico was vindictive enough on his brother's account to revenge himself by delaying the death-blow deliberately. He proved by his bearing throughout the scene that this was not so.

But whatever had happened and however bad it was, it had to be brazened out. It needed hardihood, but Christina was never lacking in this. The death of Monaldesco was a simple act of justice performed by a queen upon an unfaithful subject. As to where it was performed—that was of no consequence. It was necessary to act at once, and that Fontainebleau should be the scene of the execution was unfortunate but unavoidable.

She called it an execution, but the French Court called it murder. And not only murder, but a gross breach of hospitality—in the worst possible taste, in fact. Louis, who was about to visit her, postponed the journey indefinitely. Fontainebleau became out of bounds for the Court. Let Christina languish through the dull winter if she liked. They could not wish her a more dreary fate than to be in that palace at that time of year. As for the French Court, it fed very heartily for the rest of the winter on moral indignation, unaccustomed fare which kept it bright and lively through a season of brilliant diversions whose brilliance was heightened by the fact that Christina was not bidden to any of them. Mazarin protested hotly against her conduct; he sent Chanut to tell her she must hide the truth and blame her courtiers for the death of Monaldesco. In reply she said she would do anything for the King but repent of what she had done, and she knew of no one great or powerful enough to make her disavow her actions—that if she had not done what she had done, she would do it that night before she went to bed—that she had no reason to repent; on the contrary, she was satisfied with what she had done. These were her sentiments and if they liked them she was delighted, but if not she would continue to hold them.

The only concession she made to Mazarin was to dismiss Ludovico Santinelli and the two guards who were his accomplices. But the beloved Francesco was naturally in greater favour than ever since the cowardly attempt at mischief-making by Monaldesco. Five days after the execution she writes to him:

> I send you the story of the death of Monaldesco, who betrayed me and wanted to make me think you were the traitor. I had all the evidence necessary to prove the contrary, and I did not want to do you the injustice to believe of you the infamies of which I cannot imagine anyone but himself being capable.
>
> It was necessary for me to pretend to believe what he told me in order to justify you and to punish him.
>
> At last he died, confessing his infamy and your innocence, protesting that he had invented all these chimeras to ruin you.
>
> Note this example and pray to God that He will not deny you either brains or honour. Always behave like a gentleman and do nothing unworthy of this character.
>
> Do not trouble to justify my action to anyone. I hold myself answerable to God alone, and He would have punished me if I had pardoned this traitor's great crime. And that should be enough for you.
>
> My conscience tells me that I have acted accord-

ing to human and divine justice, and that I could not, that I should not, have done otherwise. And this is all that I can tell you.

Be contented while I do all I can to get for you the consolation you desire, and be sure I shall plead your cause.

FONTAINEBLEAU,
November 15, 1657.

The consolation Santinelli desired was a dukedom, but he did not get it.

Christina could not fail to be conscious that her presence at Fontainebleau was a nuisance, and that the most agreeable thing she could do would be to depart as soon as possible. If she did, the world would surely say that she had been asked to go, and it would be tantamount to an admission of blame, since she was here ostensibly to arrange her financial affairs, and everyone knew that her arrangements were not complete. But Fontainebleau was dull and cold, and she soon tired of exhibiting with bravado the traces of Monaldesco's murder still staining the pavement of the Galerie des Cerfs. An invitation elsewhere was the only dignified way of moving her from Fontainebleau. She fished for one from England, but Cromwell, firmly determined not to invite so dangerous a lady, returned compliment for compliment, and that was all. So there was nothing for it but to languish at Fontainebleau, and occupy herself with financial schemes and the Naples project, both of which Mazarin took up again very soon after the death of Monaldesco. By an arrangement with Charles Gustavus, she was to have a part of France's debt to Sweden. She claimed over nine hundred thousand crowns, but only succeeded in getting thirty-three thousand. As to the Naples project, Mazarin still pretended that France was interested, promising troops and battleships, and assuring her that if the enterprise succeeded, the King wished Christina to have all the honour and glory.

The rigours of Fontainebleau were endured till February, when Christina was driven to insist upon being invited to Paris, her pretext being that she was anxious to see the King in Benserade and Lully's ballet " Alcibiades ". This was unwillingly conceded, and she was lodged in Mazarin's apartment at the Louvre, an unmistakable hint that she was not expected to stay long. However, to Anne of Austria's disgust, she stayed three weeks and amused herself as best she could, going often to the play in public carriages picked up in the street, accompanied only by men. The long anticipated reception by the Académie Française was the chief event of these three weeks. It was an impulsively planned visit, and only fifteen or sixteen of the forty sages were gathered to do homage to the Sibyl of the North. They did not have time to hang the portrait Christina had presented to the Académie, as an hour was all they had to assemble the members and prepare the great salon in which she was to be received. At five in the afternoon one of her footmen announced that she had arrived, and her carriage was heard down below in the Louvre courtyard. She was accompanied by Madame de Brègy, whose husband was French Ambassador in Poland. Her first question was whether the academicians stood up or sat in her presence. The precedent of Charles IX's visit in the time of Ronsard was brought forward. They could be seated. A long session followed in which a quantity of verses were read, after which the director, M. de Chambre, said that the Académie was much occupied in preparing his dictionary, and would Her Majesty be so gracious as to hear an extract from it? Her Majesty having consented, Mezerai opened the dictionary apparently at random at the word " *Jeu* " and read the following:

" *Jeux des princes qui ne plaisent qu'à ceux qui les font. Pour exprimer les actes de violence exerçés par les hommes revêtus du pouvoir suprême.*"

Christina laughed heartily at this, some say to cover her confusion and blushes, but it is not likely that she was ever confused or ever blushed. The reading of " *Jeu* " took an hour, after which Christina rose, and bowing profoundly to the company, left the way she came. Soon afterwards she quitted Paris and went on her way to Toulon. Gui Patin writes: " She is gone away ill-pleased with the Queen, having heard that she had said if the Queen of Sweden did not go, she would herself leave the Louvre." Her usual route through Savoy was barred to her because by now her Naples project was well known. French warships carried her and her suite to Leghorn. They were transporting troops to the Duke of Modena. On the 7th of May she met the Duke and they signed a treaty for the invasion of Naples.

PART III

CARDINAL RED

CHAPTER XII

PALAZZO RIARIO

THE treaty with the Duke of Modena, for all the solemnity of its signing, was so much waste paper. One of the clauses was that Christina should obtain the Pope's sanction for the free passage of the Duke's armies through the Papal States. This in itself was enough to damn the whole project, and Alexander had no desire to support the plot against Spain.

When, in the spring of 1658, Christina returned to Rome, the Pope's attitude towards her was clearly demonstrated by his refusal to leave his summer quarters at Castel Gandolfo,[1] to welcome her back to the city. He contented himself with the gift of a handsome *rinfresco*—a good show of wine, game, fruits and other delicacies, carried by no less than twenty-four *facchini*.

" Ha! " cried Christina at this. " In Rome it seems they provision the enemy before the siege! "

The Farnese Palace was not available. The Duke of Parma had seen to that. Christina borrowed Mazarin's residence, which was in the same piazza as the pontifical Quirinal—another source of irritation to the Pope. Gossip said she was enrolling her troops there, and so disquieting were the tales brought to His Holiness that he had the

[1] Still the Pope's summer residence to which has lately been added the neighbouring Villa Barberini.

Palace heavily guarded and patrolled night and day. Christina's reply to this was to dismiss most of her own guard, seeing that the Pope was looking after her so well.

The Naples project languished through the summer, and finally flickered out with the death of the Duke of Modena in October, by which time Christina was busy with other devices to pass the time and spend money. She had for a long time been pondering on the Turkish menace to Europe, and she had enough vision to conceive the idea of a union of Christian nations, a crusade against the invasion of the infidel. The seed of this grand scheme lay in a project of hers for reinstating Ludovico Santinelli, the executioner of Monaldesco, who was waiting at Modena until the Fontainebleau incident should cease to be the principal topic of Rome. He should lead an army against the Turks, under the Venetian standard!

Probably no one less appropriate than Ludovico could have been chosen for this high rôle, but Christina threw herself into the plan with her usual enthusiasm, discussing it fervently with the Venetian Ambassador, who seems to have taken it seriously, and even advancing three thousand crowns of her own money for preliminary expenses. Then suddenly the whole thing came to nothing, and Ludovico is not heard of again. The Crusade idea, however, was not entirely abandoned, and hung like a rich tapestry behind the inconsequent tangle of ambitious schemes and erratic notions which cluttered the foreground of her mind. Though it was as abortive as the rest, there was grandeur in its conception, and it is unique among her schemes in being directed towards the good of the Church and Europe more than towards her own self-aggrandisement.

The usual financial exasperations greeted her in Rome. She had borrowed a largish sum from Cardinal Mazarin when in France, besides the thirty-three thousand crowns which he had added to her revenue through Sweden. She had entrusted the payment of this debt to her agent Texiera, who had fulfilled his trust with such dismaying alacrity that she found a meagre sum awaiting her in Rome; and to add to her anxieties, her emissary Davidsson, a convert to the Faith, returned from Sweden with the worst possible bulletin of her financial position, and of his reception in Sweden. The King's horror of Catholics was such that he had refused to interview him. Besides which, he was so much occupied with complicated military operations that Christina's demands, always irksome, were scarcely to be thought of.

She was so incensed by the apparent indifference to her interests in one who owed so much to her, that she wrote him a long, very forcible letter reproaching him for his neglect and, urged as usual by the necessity for ready money, suggesting the sale outright of one of her towns, Norrköping, to be paid for by Sweden from the subsidies due from France in virtue of the new alliance.

But Charles was not really callous. In the face of the continual opposition of his advisers, the devastation of her lands in Pomerania, and the grave situation of Sweden, he spared her what he could from the exhausted treasury. Mazarin, continually being importuned for funds, at last definitely refused to supply her with another crown, on the grounds that he could do nothing without the consent of Sweden. Finally, Texiera in Hamburg was able to lend a respectable sum on her jewels, which had not been fully pledged.

Meanwhile, pawning and selling were the order of the day. Francesco Santinelli, still Grand Chamberlain, busied himself with the disposal of plate, bibelots, tapestries and embroideries; even her mantle of State with its gold crowns and ermine lining went the way of the rest. Experience had taught Francesco all there was to know about the art of plundering, and so blindly did Christina trust him now, as if to compensate him for the treachery of Monaldesco, that the tricks he played upon her were such as should not have deceived a child. Her diamonds, he said, were still in pawn, because the money she had given him to redeem them he had lent to Cardinal Azzolino, who was so sensitive about the transaction that it would be better not to mention it to him. All the liveries, uniforms and arms that she had brought from Paris for her entry into Naples were borrowed ostensibly for theatricals, but they were never seen again. She questioned nothing, but that was her way. When a person was in favour he could do no wrong. As soon as his usefulness or charm began to wear thin, he could do nothing right. Monaldesco was the extreme case of this extravagant taking up and dropping of persons and projects.

While Christina was in France and Francesco Santinelli was supposed to be looking after her interests in Rome, Donna Anna Maria Aldobrandini, the grand-niece of Clement VIII and the wealthy young widow of the Duke of Ceri, appeared upon the scene. She fell in love with Santinelli, but when she announced that she was going to marry him, her family raised strong objections to the penniless provincial nobleman whose character was only too well known in Rome. There was even a rumour, none too vague, that he had poisoned the Duke of Ceri with the help of the Duchess. The family appealed to the Pope to forbid the marriage. Alexander took up the charge vigorously, and the affair had arrived at this stage when Christina returned to Rome. The lovers at once enlisted her sympathy. She was ready to give it to any cause Santinelli might have at heart, and she loved an intrigue, especially if there was passion in it. She wrote at once to the Duke of Parma, who was a relation of the Duchess, asking for his support. The Pope was very angry at this; the Duchess was sent under an armed guard to a convent, and the dismissal of Santinelli was demanded of Christina.

Convent bars, not too forbidding, only made the affair more interesting, and if anything were needed to keep the lovers at fever heat, Christina supplied it with continual admonitions and encouragements, and the designing of a plot to spirit away the Duchess from the convent and marry the pair secretly. But the Pope had as many spies in the convent as the Ceri had friends, and he was perfectly aware of every development. Just as the plot was matured, the lady disappeared. She was imprisoned in Castello Sant' Angelo, where, though she was comfortably lodged she was completely cut off from the world, and so carefully watched that the most ardent lover could not so much as smuggle a note.

The fun of fighting His Holiness soon began to pall. After all, he was Head of the Church, however irrational he might be, and it was humiliating to be kept waiting for an audience, as Christina was for several weeks. Not easy to retaliate on this. At last an audience was granted, but it was a frigid affair. All the cordiality had gone out of their relations. Alexander had complained that she was a barbarian, that her ideas were barbarian, and that her pride was ferocious, almost intolerable. He had sent out two ultimatums to her as soon as she arrived in Rome. First, that she should dismiss Santinelli from her service immediately, and secondly, that she should change her residence at once. She did neither, for the moment. Alexander was accustomed to be obeyed; he became more and more exasperated, and the Ceri business was the final exasperation. Cardinal de Retz wrote of Alexander VII:

> He is a man of minutiæ, which is not only a sign of a small mind, but of a mean spirit. He told me one day of his youthful studies, and how for two years he used the same pen; this is only a bagatelle, but, as I have often remarked, it is the little things that matter and not the big ones; it did not please me.

Wise counsels prevailed with Christina at last, and they came from Azzolino. The first move was the evacuation of the Palazzo Mazarin. She retired into a convent for a short while, and the world said that she was going to take the veil. While the Duchess of Ceri was incarcerated in Sant' Angelo Christina wrote a letter of sober advice to her, urging her to give up Santinelli. This was for the eyes of the Pope, who took it for what it was, another drop of balm which at Azzolino's suggestion she was applying to his ruffled feelings. And, yes, even Santinelli should go, but only as far as Vienna to carry her compliments to the Emperor, Leopold the Great, and sound him on the possibility of his lending her twenty thousand troops under Montecuculi, that she might wrest from Sweden the land of Pomerania, where she had so many supporters, and serve Charles Gustavus right for his neglect. Whatever Santinelli achieved on this question—there is only one letter from him and that is in cipher—he found Vienna sufficiently diverting, and Christina reproaches him with staying too long, and accepting far more entertainment than his position warranted. Another letter from her, dated May 13, 1659, shows that she has discovered he is posing as her ambassador in Vienna. " Which is far from being your standing, and farther still from your deserts." She declares that she is disgusted with his follies, and, in short, gives him formal notice to quit her service.

Events had moved quickly after his departure for

Vienna. A horrible tragedy was the burning of Christina's stables through the carelessness of her French coachman. All her splendid horses perished and most of her equipages.

Palazzo Riario, on the Lungara near the Porta San Pancrazio, by the death of the Princess Botero, fell vacant, and Christina bought it. The lease was signed by Cardinal Barberini, who advanced money for the purchase. The Pope, now full of graciousness, appointed Cardinal Azzolino to be director of her household. It did not take the Cardinal long to convince her of her late Chamberlain's villainy. His absence laid bare his atrocious frauds. Azzolino laughed at the story of the diamonds and the borrowed money. It was not difficult for her to write that letter of dismissal to Santinelli. He was most definitely finished, and there is no record of her ever seeing him again.

Palazzo Riario, which is now the Corsini, became Christina's headquarters until her death. At last she had found the home she wanted. It would hold all her treasures and it had a most delicious garden. The transport of her library and other possessions from Antwerp was put in train at once. Azzolino devoted himself with such enthusiasm to the adjustment of her affairs that a reasonable and even dignified life seemed to be before her. There was not a taint of Santinelli left in her household when the Cardinal had cleared up the dreadful disorder above and below stairs.

He gave her an establishment worthy of her status, but not too costly. There were twenty gentlemen, a good show of lackeys and pages, and among the members of her suite was the Abbé Santini, who took the place of Santinelli's friend and accomplice, Baschi, as her secretary. Santini was a fine fellow, devoted to Azzolino and Christina, a linguist with an exquisite hand, somewhat addicted to wine and not at all indifferent to women. He, and the

Canon de Marchis, her majordomo, were in her service till her death, and Macchiati, her doctor, who came from Azzolino's birthplace, and Pezza, her librarian, died in her service. Lorenzo Adami, also from Fermo, was Captain of the Guard. She was surrounded now by decent people, and for the rest of her life a small band of affectionate servitors and friends faithfully bore with her egotism and vagaries, for the sake of the generous heart that never really changed.

Peace of mind came to Christina, much as in the old days when Bourdelot came to Stockholm. This time it was not overwork, but the haunting consciousness of the muddle she had made of her emancipation, that had brought her spirits low. And, instead of Bourdelot, Azzolino was the healer. She changed her ways; the arrogant pride which had so shocked Rome last year had given place to an agreeable manner. She was sprightly and cheerful; someone said that she combined French vivacity, Italian wit, Swedish courage and Roman good manners. She began her studies again, and wasted a good deal of time and money in her laboratory trying to turn base metal into gold. . . .

She was a happy woman because at last she was really in love, and the man she loved was constantly beside her. She was now thirty-two, and Azzolino was only three years older.

Every day her private chamber in the Riario would be illuminated by this enthralling personality. They would sit side by side, poring over the details of her household—and no one should say more than that the Queen and Azzolino were occupied with household affairs. It was his duty to come to her and it was her ever-growing pleasure to receive him. There was the flash and challenge of brilliant dark eyes to radiant blue eyes—the accidental touch of slim, eloquent hand on shapely boy's hand, as papers were passed or a book consulted. Rich, alluring silences when thought met thought and not a word was spoken! Here was the perfect Latin—realist, poet, dreamer, worker and lover. Here, indeed, was the man of men, the great one, controller of her destiny.

Happy and at peace though she was under Azzolino's domination, for it amounted to that, one weakness in her character was fostered by his influence. She had never really loved her country, and her persistent demands for more revenue in the face of the tragic situation in Sweden, the fierce insistence on her rights, were encouraged by the Cardinal, who had no objection to fleecing a Protestant country which had tried, but failed, to subdue Catholic Poland.

In 1659 Sweden was without allies, at war with the Empire, Poland, Denmark and Russia. Charles Gustavus, always at the head of his troops, led them through stirring feats of war, but failure dogged the gallant leader. There was the historic march of the entire army over the frozen Baltic in February, 1658, when, Terlon, the French Ambassador, who accompanied Charles, says: "It was horror to walk at night across the frozen sea; the horses' tramping had thawed the snow so that the water rose one or two feet on the ice; every moment we feared to find the sea open somewhere to engulf us." Though the Danes sued for peace after this almost miraculous invasion and a pact was made, it was soon broken, and fighting became so ferocious that the Dutch fleet intervened on behalf of Denmark, and an English fleet arrived to attempt mediation. The English Ambassador, Algernon Sidney, called on Charles at his camp and annoyed him by trying to dictate terms. So did the Dutch Ambassador. But almost simultaneously these two fleets were called away, the Dutch to transport Danish armies to a defeat of the Swedish troops elsewhere, and the English to take part in the restoration of King Charles II of England. Charles Gustavus, undaunted, began to raise more troops and funds at Gothenburg. In the midst of these preparations he died quite suddenly of a fever, aged thirty-seven, on February 13, 1660.

Charles was dead! The worst, from Christina's point of view, had happened. The news, which took two months to reach Rome, shattered the Riario idyll. However unsatisfactory her cousin's efforts may have been to meet her demands, they were at least efforts—she had known that his goodwill was there. But now—who was there to care for her interests? Who, indeed, that was not indifferent or actively hostile? The new King was only five years old. There would be a regency as in her own day. Of whom would it consist? The sinister figure of Magnus de la Gardie loomed. As uncle by marriage to the young King he was sure to hold high office, and there was not much doubt that his revengeful spirit had already been at work against her.

The peaceful existence at Palazzo Riario had in truth begun to pall, in spite of entertainments, academies and the ever-present and ever-more adored Azzolino; and the death of Charles made it really imperative that she should set out again on her feverish travels. There were no two opinions about it, she must go to Hamburg, if not to Stockholm, and preparations went forward at once for her departure with a small suite.

The pretext upon which she had sent Santinelli to Vienna was, after all, a genuine one. She really had contemplated leading an imperial army into her own province of Pomerania, if the Emperor would provide it for her.

Then she would enjoy the revenue from this unhappy devastated land, and it should revert to the Emperor at her death. This blow aimed at her native land could only have been inspired by pique at Charles's apparent neglect, and the affair had so far developed that she had been already making tentative arrangements to go to Hamburg and meet an emissary from the Emperor, even, though she did not know it, after the death of Charles.

She set forth from Rome in July, 1660, having borrowed twenty thousand crowns on her jewellery from the Pope, who gave her a short, frosty audience of *congé*. Azzolino was left in charge of the Riario and all her affairs, and she took with her the Captain of her Guards, Lorenzo Adami, her doctor, Macchiati, three secretaries, Davidsson the Swede, the Abbé Santini and Benedetto Rossi, the invaluable Clairet Poisonnet and her two faithful Italian women, and a dozen or so domestics.

At Trent Horatio de Bourbon, Marquis del Monte, who was an exile from the Papal States, came to ask Christina for her protection. The Bourbons of Italy bore the arms of the royal family of France, and traced their pedigree back to Charlemagne. Their estates were in the Apennine Mountains, remotely inaccessible, the haunt of bandits whom rumour said were not merely protected by this noble impoverished family. However that may have been, the Marquis joined Christina's suite, travelled with her to Hamburg, and eventually became her Master of the Horse. A contemporary portrait of him describes him as " a proper man of handsome Shape; had a large Face, hollow Eyes, a hooked Nose, a large Mouth and a forked Chin. He was nervous and of a strong Constitution, having his Body Hairy, his Knees turning outward and his Feet inward; a Person very sensible, but more inclined to Ill than Good; Passionate in Play, and knew all the Tricks and Cheats thereof. . . . He knew when to Speak and when to be Silent . . . was very brisk among the ladies, and spent much money upon them ".

With this notable addition to her suite she arrived in Hamburg on the 18th of August. There was no envoy from Vienna waiting for her, and this was not surprising, as the Empire had made peace with Sweden on the 26th of April without consulting her. So the Pomeranian project ended in smoke. It did not matter, for she was now engrossed in the prospect of visiting Stockholm and had all sorts of surprises up her sleeve. Stockholm was quite prepared for this, and, not wanting any surprises, tried to persuade her not to come. The danger of Christina's presence at this critical period was fully realized by the Regency. The King was a delicate child, and if he did not live the question of succession came up again, and it was well known in Sweden that Christina had an enormous following among her late subjects, and there was no knowing what she might not accomplish if she had a mind to return to the throne. She was capable of renouncing her faith if it suited her, and, if she did so, would remove the only serious obstacle to her reinstatement. Here they misjudged her, for the one rock she clung to through life was her faith.

She waited in Hamburg to hear how Sweden took the news of her intended visit. The response was not encouraging. The Governor-General of her Swedish domains, Bååt, regretted to inform her that the idea was not well seen, and Pierre Brahe who had once refused to take the crown from her head, begged her to reconsider her plans.

But no one could prevent Christina from going to Sweden if she wanted to, and by the time these chilling messages arrived her mind was warmly and unalterably fixed upon the journey. She took Terlon, the French

Ambassador, with her, and in Denmark, the ink of the peace pact being scarcely dry as yet, and Christina an unknown quantity in the new Swedish situation, she was magnificently received by the King and his Queen, Sophie Amalie. The incident of a country inn some years ago was not mentioned. She was taken across to Helsingborg in the King's galley, which, after depositing her, was broken into a thousand pieces by a storm on the way back to Denmark. At Helsingborg she wrote to Brahe that she was in despair at not being able to follow his advice about coming to Sweden, but in short here she was, and with the best possible intentions. There was consternation in the Regency when the news came that she had really landed. A last effort to dissuade her from her purpose was made by one Marshal Linde, who was ostensibly sent to greet her in the name of the King at Halmstad, an early stage of her journey. His instructions were to use all possible diplomacy—suggest that there might be serious trouble if she persisted in visiting Stockholm. At this she was indignant and sent him about his business, pressing on with renewed determination towards Stockholm. The fighting blood of the Vasas was roused. Now let the Regency take heed!

CHAPTER XIII

THE REGENCY

THE leading personality in the Regency was Christina's old favourite and enemy, Magnus de la Gardie. He was now a commanding figure in Swedish politics. His youthful good looks had matured to remarkable distinction, and the dash of French blood gave him that elegance which his compeers lacked. The Queen-Mother and Prince Adolphus were secondary figures, but they were unanimous in the decision that, since Christina was here, there was nothing to be done but to receive her with all the superficial honours that were her due. She entered Stockholm in state and was led by the boy King to her own apartments in the Palace, which he had given up to her.

Almost her first act was to turn one of the rooms into a chapel, where Mass was immediately celebrated with as much publicity as possible. There was bravado in the manner of asserting her faith without regard to the sentiments of her Lutheran hosts, but it served only to give the Regency just the pretext they needed for incommoding her. Their first move was to insist upon the departure of the Italians of her suite, including the Abbé Santini, her chaplain, on the grounds that besides being Papists, they were people of scandalous behaviour. She was obliged to give way to this, and sent them to Hamburg, where they awaited her return.

The Senate was not long left in doubt as to the principal object of her visit. It was to confirm the decrees passed at her abdication with regard to her revenues—to ensure, in fact, that under the new order of things she would not lose what so far she had never really succeeded in getting. The first issue was with the clergy, who seized this opportunity of stating to her what they had been thinking ever since her conversion, that according to the decrees of Gustavus, her grandfather, whoever deserted the Faith for Popery should renounce inheritance and all rights and privileges whatsoever in the realm of Sweden. However, because she was her father's daughter and for the sake of her illustrious ancestors, they were prepared to concede the revenues originally promised as an act of grace.

But the chapel, which was opposite the apartment of the young King, must be instantly dismantled. There must be no exercise of Popery in public or in secret while she was a guest in the Palace. Christina wept; but the chapel was dismantled. Now it was her turn.

On the 16th of November the Senate received with amazement a document in her own hand, wherein she declared that, if the present King died without heirs, she had the right to the throne, and no one could deprive her of it. This bomb, which was really no more than a firework, dropped into the midst of the assembly just when it thought Christina and her affairs were settled, was returned to her still smoking within an hour. The King was a sickly child, and a frail buffer between Christina and the crown if she meant to have it. A second Act of Renunciation was hastily drawn up, in which she abandoned once and for all any claim to the throne of Sweden. This she was obliged to sign, while Magnus de la Gardie stood by, with his courtly manner and malicious smile.

Though she was ever missing a crown on her head, her wish to reign again in Sweden was only momentary. Something had to be done to startle the Senate, and she had certainly succeeded in doing that. A gracious Act of Renunciation, however, with an heroic background, was a very different thing from this emergency document forced upon her by a hostile Regency. She was wretched in Stockholm, but her financial affairs were not securely settled yet, and she would not leave Sweden until they were. She spent Christmas in the capital, hearing Mass at M. Terlon's house and communicating as publicly as possible. In the new year she moved to her own town of Norrköping, accompanied by Terlon, who, when he returned to Stockholm, left his chaplain, Vacquier, in the Queen's temporary service. Here Galeazzo Gualdo arrived from France, where he had spent a year trying to negotiate money advances for her with but little success. Then there were more Turco-Venetian dreams, for Gualdo, who was a Venetian, brought her messages from the Republic asking for help against the infidel.

In the four months that she was at Norrköping she was planning vast schemes—the Crusade, Catholic liberty in the North, and other high matters before which the throne of Sweden faded into insignificance. Whatever her schemes were, her ultimate goal was always Rome, and her desire to leave Sweden acute. She writes at the end of a letter to her secretary, Davidsson, in Hamburg:

"You will see me in Hamburg when I think it advisable, or rather when my affairs allow it; because you know that, if I let them out of my sight without having put the last touches, all the trouble I have taken will be wasted." She bids him "console my poor Italians" and says that her desire is to return to Rome as soon as possible.

It was impossible for Christina to be anywhere, least of

all in Sweden, without stirring up discord. Her stormy petrel personality was bound to create factions, and the Regency saw real danger in her provocative presence in the realm. She was therefore attacked continually at her most vulnerable point—her religion. Though there was no interference with Catholic representatives of foreign countries, Christina and her suite were embarrassed to an extent that almost amounted to persecution. Vacquier, the chaplain, was ordered to leave her, though there had been no objection to him when he was with Terlon. An accumulation of offensive measures brought her to desperation, and in March she wrote to her Governor-General, Bååt:

> For God's sake make haste to settle my affairs, so that I can leave as soon as possible this country where I am so cruelly persecuted, because I assure you that as soon as I get my money I shall not stay in this place an hour, and I would rather die miserably elsewhere than live in Sweden subjected to daily insults. . . .

In April, 1661, her affairs were apparently in order, but she could not escape without being entertained by the Regency, who throughout the process of attrition had observed all the outward forms of friendliness. On the 13th of April she wrote to Prince Adolphus to try and excuse herself from attending the fête he proposed in her honour, as she had at all costs to go immediately to Hamburg, but a second note from her six days later shows that the Prince was so persistent in his invitation that she had to yield. There was scarcely a hint of triumph in de la Gardie's courtly farewell. Magnificent, unassailable, he could wait. His revenge was cumulative—no sudden stroke, that was not his way—just a series of discomforts so that her life in Rome, or wherever she chose to be, should never be quite free from preoccupations.

She was as glad to leave Sweden as she had been six years ago, and gladder still to get back to her "poor Italians" who greeted her with such genuine pleasure when she arrived at last in Hamburg. Here she was obliged to remain for a year, chiefly engaged in organizing her financial affairs with the Jew, Texiera. He now became sole administrator of her Swedish funds, and an elaborate contract was drawn up whereby he was to be gradually paid back all the large sums he had lent her from time to time, and on his side he was to ensure her a certain income of eight thousand crowns a month. This was all on the assumption that her Swedish funds would now be regularly forthcoming.

The idea of Catholic liberty was again taken up with enthusiasm. She wrote to all the Catholic rulers inviting their interest in the scheme. Gualdo was rushed off to France to put the matter before Louis XIV. Louis temporized, not wanting to offend Christina. The Emperor Leopold of Austria definitely refused to have anything to do with it, foreseeing a similar indulgence being demanded of himself for Protestants in his own realm. The King of Poland was discouraging, and Philip of Spain left his answer so late that it did not come until the idea had vanished into smoke. At any rate Rome would hear of Christina's efforts and applaud them. These exercises in *haute politique* kept her mind and pen busy, and if they wasted other people's time they served to stir things up.

There was nothing that had happened since she left Rome which was not known to Azzolino. She herself wrote him long, intimate letters, and her secretaries kept him minutely informed of every detail of her life. He was waiting for her at Terni when she arrived from

Hamburg. Outside Rome she was met by one of the Chigi cardinals, who took her straight to the Vatican where she kissed the Pope's toe. Her costume for this ceremony was remarkable. Her hair was tied up with a disorderly arrangement of different coloured ribbons; her head was powdered, not by art, but by the dusty roads round Rome; a veil was attached to the back of her neck and drawn under one arm. With her usual *just-au-corps* she wore a transparent skirt through which her riding breeches could be plainly discerned.

But however attired, she was welcomed with enthusiasm by Alexander. So far as he knew there were no projects in the air to embroil him, and the news of her financial adjustments had expanded his heart with goodwill and friendliness. She went straight to the Palazzo Riario after this interview, but, though an immense amount of work had been done to it in the last year, it was not quite ready for her. Azzolino had prepared a small pavilion as a temporary residence on the Gianicolo, where the statue of Garibaldi now stands. Here she lived for the rest of the year. The Turco-Venetian project came up again. Gualdo was at hand to spur her on, and the Venetian Ambassador supported him. Christina determined to raise a regiment herself. For this her jewellery should be sold; it was worth three hundred thousand crowns, and only forty-six thousand would be needed to reclaim it from pawn. If she raised a regiment it would inspire other Christian princes.

A bitter disappointment awaited her. In spite of her efforts at Stockholm, Texiera wrote complaining that her revenue was not coming in from Sweden, and that instead of her debt to him diminishing it was increasing. Azzolino's feelings at this news must have been mixed. He was looking forward to a properly organized and securely established household at last for Christina on the strength of the Texiera contract. But if the Crusade materialized, there was no guessing where the spate of expenditure would end. The news from Hamburg at least stemmed the tide. Meanwhile, he and Santini were engaged with Christina in preparing the ninety-eight missives which were to be distributed personally throughout Catholic Europe by Galeazzo Gualdo. They were drafted in French by Christina. Azzolino was responsible for the Italian, and all were transcribed in Santini's exquisite hand.

Gualdo set off on his mission in August, 1662. Though he was Christina's envoy, for some reason he had not the full authority of the Venetian Republic, and he was suspiciously regarded because of his lack of papers. He was away no less than eighteen months, but as far as the Crusade was concerned he came back empty-handed, and the rich dream tapestry at the back of Christina's mind faded again. The Doge had had little belief in the enterprise from the first, and though the Venetian Ambassador wrote indignantly, "*La Reine entreprend les choses et puis les abandonne au beau milieu*", in this case it was not so much her caprice as force of circumstances and the ineffectiveness of Gualdo that defeated it.

The Duc de Crequi came to Rome as French Ambassador at this time. France had withdrawn her embassy in 1653, so the arrival of the new Minister was a delicate step towards better relations between the Vatican and Louis XIV. Crequi was a pompous person whose rigid insistence on his own rights in matters of etiquette was above the ordinary. First he denied that it was his duty to pay his respects to the Pope's relations, the Cardinals Chigi, and then he obstinately refused to visit Christina unless he were given an armchair at the audience. Now, in Christina's audience chamber, armchairs were reserved exclusively for cardinals, and a stool was all Crequi would have to sit on if he called. Christina was firm. A stool or no audience.

Details of this foolish little storm were immediately sent to M. de Lionne in Paris, and to the King himself, by Azzolino. Christina also wrote to Louis, on June 27, 1662. It was a charming letter, and it declared how much she had looked forward to greeting his ambassador, but alas, that circumstances should prevent her from proclaiming her affection and respect for the beloved monarch. She begs him to order his ambassador not to ask impossible things, since she is convinced that he is still more interested in herself than in his ambassador.

The answer came swiftly. M. le Duc must sit on a stool. He obeyed with as good a grace as he could muster, and a few days later came an order from the King that he was to visit the Cardinals Chigi. The humiliating calls were paid, and all Rome laughed. There the affair should have ended, a diverting little comedy of manners.

But one night in August a party of the Duke's household was attacked by some of the Pope's Corsican Guard. No one ever knew who was the instigator of the attack, but as Cardinal Mario Chigi, the Pope's brother, was responsible for the Corsican Guard, he was not above suspicion. The Frenchmen fled to the Farnese Palace where the Ambassador lodged, pursued by Corsicans, who attacked the Palace with a discharge of musketry, barely missing the Ambassador himself, who stepped out on the balcony to find out what the noise was about. The Duchess, at this moment returning in her carriage from some entertainment, was attacked and one of her pages killed.

This very grave incident roused Christina to frenzied action. She immediately sent a message to the Farnese offering her help; she arranged a visit from Cardinal Mario Chigi to the Duke, and she tried to impress upon the Pope the urgency of giving prompt satisfaction to France. In a note to Azzolino she says that she wrote to the Duke begging him to prevent his messenger from leaving for Paris until the ill had been remedied.

> When it is over the Pope will realize that I have done an important service in this affair. Once more, I implore you to persuade him to give satisfaction to the Ambassador at once, because if he does not, I can foresee grave trouble. One of the Corsicans must be sacrificed, and if the real culprit is not found, then the innocent must be punished, to show that they are not being shielded and that no tricks have been used to spare them. What I say to you seems terrible, but extreme cases require extreme remedies.

The barbarous suggestion of the Northern Queen did not appeal to Alexander, who did nothing decisive, lacking vision and initiative, and fearing to probe the affair too deeply on account of his brother's possible complicity. France made it clear that full satisfaction would be demanded for the insult to her Minister and his lady, and as still Alexander hesitated, Crequi was recalled, and what Christina predicted happened. After months of negotiation and threats of invasion by France, the Pope was forced to sign the treaty of Pisa, Cardinal Flavio Chigi, his nephew, was sent to Paris bearing the Papal apologies to the King, and the Corsican Guards were abolished, a monument being erected in the place of their guard-house, with an inscription in Latin and French describing their crime and humiliation. This monument was demolished three years later.

Throughout the long and tedious quarrel Christina was writing letters to Louis, defending, as far as it was possible, the Pope, even his nepotism, which Louis had attacked, and with good reason, for it was generally admitted that the number of Alexander's relations wearing cardinals' hats was excessive. Louis became colder and more ironical as the correspondence grew, and the ultimate importance of the Crequi incident to her was the temporary loss of Louis's friendship, which was especially precious now that France and Sweden were in close alliance. It was not until 1665 that she and Louis were at peace again, chiefly because, the Pope having shown sign of failing health, Louis saw the advantage of being on good terms with Azzolino, who would obviously be one of the important figures in the next conclave, and perhaps, if sufficiently caressed, disposed to favour France, which had been sadly used by the Vatican.

The Riario was ready in January, 1662, and Christina found herself at last in a perfect background surrounded by her treasures, her magnificent library housed, her tapestries, her Correggios and the rest of her pictures adequately hung.

Flowers and shrubs filled the gardens; the shaded walks were rich with statuary; orange and lemon groves were planted. The stables were filled with horses, Turco, the Queen's favourite saddle horse, Argentino, Ballerino, Tassetto, Pallotino, Garsetto, Garaffa, Scarpaccia, Caporale, Gioia, Malatesta, Arabo, Capitano, Buffone, Belladonna, Campione, Baiard, Montedoro, Rodomonte, Cervio, Spada, Cappa Serpentino, Gesuito. An important addition to her suite was the Duke of Poli, of the great Conti family. He was described as " a big man, very gross, whose age made him grow stooping. He was certainly a Lord of Merit, full of Honour, and incorruptible Probity, reserved in discourse, and Phegmatick to the uttermost point; he would always say that everything was brought to pass with Patience. He was as severe as Cato; and as to his Economy, it would have been called sparing in another, who had not been charged with so great a number of children."

As he was one of the first gentlemen of Rome, Christina was delighted to have him in her service, though patience and economy were not qualities that appealed to her. The Duchess was lady-in-waiting, but her services were never required except at feasts, and there were no women but her faithful Italian maids about the Queen.

Among her secretaries was young Count d'Alibert, a Frenchman who first attracted Christina's attention at carnival time, when in a procession which she was watching from her window he appeared as Apollo in a gorgeous chariot representing Mount Parnassus with the Nine Muses and a concert of instruments making a fine symphony. He was afterwards admitted to her presence, and very soon was established as her Secretary of Embassies. He must have had a good deal of the easy charm that so delighted Christina in the Santinellis, and she enjoyed his chatter and nonsense. He had a gift for organizing amusement, and among his activities were a comedy theatre at the Torre di Nona, a tennis-court near the Piazza di Spagna, and several gaming-houses. Christina sent him as ambassador of peace to Louis XIV when the Crequi affair was at its worst, but he was soon sent back with an ironical note from the King.

These four years, from 1662 to 1666, were, but for the eternal money question, tranquil and happy. Texiera, it is true, sent continual complaints of the slow, feeble trickle of funds from Sweden, and after the second year of his contract with her he had to reduce her monthly income from eight thousand crowns to five thousand. Azzolino worked himself more strenuously than ever for the decent and economical maintenance of her little Court, and, with him always at hand, and the knowledge of his complete devotion to her interests, her life was almost unclouded.

The Pope paid her a visit. Since the cooling of her relations with France, Alexander's heart had warmed towards her, and this visit to the Riario was a signal for all Rome to be at her doors. But still the ladies were only accommodated with cushions if with anything at all, for Christina continued to receive them standing, and as before cleared the floor for the men. But she did not suffer bores of any kind, male or female. To one, who remarked on her love of solitude, she simply said:

"Better three days alone than half an hour with you."

A great deal of the solitude at which this courtier marvelled was passed in her laboratory, where she would spend hours filtering and distilling, trying to make the gold she so sorely needed, but only pouring out too much of what she had on expensive equipment, drugs, quicksilver and the like, and being disgracefully cheated by her assistant chemist, Bandiere. Though he made enormous profits by roguery, his life was not an enviable one, for Christina would keep him up all night at the furnaces, as this was her time of leisure, and his continued failure to produce anything that faintly resembled gold often brought pots and pans hurtling at his head and a vigorous bastinado from the Queen herself. When Azzolino discovered the dishonesty of Bandiere, he insisted upon his being paid a monthly wage and two hundred pistoles for the distillation expenses, but the astute creature was too much even for Azzolino, and the expenses became so shattering that even Christina was shocked and gave up chemistry for a time. But she did not dismiss Bandiere, who turned his talents to spying, tale-bearing and blackmailing among her suite, until finally Azzolino, exasperated by the presence of the low creature about the Queen, gave him the rope to hang himself in the shape of the monthly distribution of alms among the deserving poor, which it was Christina's habit to dispense. Naturally the deserving poor got none of it, but it was a long time before Christina would accept the assurance of Azzolino that the receipts were forged, and that most of the alms had gone to nymphs of the Settignana Gate.

Italy does not reveal her inmost self at once, though superficially she may give that impression. The midday glamour that blinds and delightfully confuses is all she gives to her casual visitor; he goes ecstatically home to the North with a burden of spurious souvenirs which have suited the irresponsible moment, but he does not know Italy. For Christina the tourist spirit was dead. Her collection of counterfeits was cast away—the Santinellis, Monaldesco, and their crew—and now the fine flower of Italy was hers; the South held her in thrall for the rest of her life.

Now it was not of Italy that Christina must beware, but of her own people. The administration of her Swedish property was not merely careless; it was criminal. Not one of the governors of her various domains protected her interests in the slightest degree. They did not trouble to collect the revenues which were her due, and most of them, especially Appelmann who governed Pomerania, lived like princes on the money that should have been hers. No wonder that one of Christina's axioms was:

" On change de voleurs en changeant de ministres. Il y a des exceptions a cette régle, mais assez rare."

One of the exceptions was Lorenzo Adami, her Captain of the Guard. He was chosen by Christina to go to Hamburg and Sweden to interview Texiera and to examine the accounts of her governors, and remedy, if possible, the hopeless state of her finances. In spite of the fact that all his business was done through an interpreter, he made himself complete master of the situation, and his correspondence with Azzolino showed on either side how whole-hearted was their loyalty to Christina. Adami did splendid and fearless work in the domains; his scheme was to let the three islands, Öland, Gottland and Ösel, which so far had been entirely unprofitable, to the highest bidders, who, taking the revenue themselves, were to pay handsome rents annually to Texiera. Appelmann was terrified into guaranteeing thirty thousand crowns from Pomerania, and Norrköping was to yield twenty thousand. This was only part of Adami's mission, and the rest of it was political. He discovered that there was a large party in the Senate that had disapproved of the rigorous treatment of Christina on her last visit, and of the conclusions of the Secret Commission which was held in 1664 to consider the possibility of her return. If she did propose to come back, she was to be forbidden to practise her religion, neither a priest nor a chapel would be allowed her, and she must not be in Stockholm if the Diet was sitting. There must be nothing but Lutherans in her Court. Her return was eagerly awaited by many; and, most interesting of all, he was able to send by her secretary, Stropp, not only the details of his activities in her domains, but the information that the Regency intended to hold an extraordinary Diet in June.

All this news, culminating in the prospect of a Diet, decided Christina. The time had come for another journey.

CHAPTER XIV

FROST

On the 22nd of May, 1666, a long line of coaches were drawn up on the Lungara, outside the Palazzo Riario. The Chigi family and other cardinals were waiting to escort Christina outside the walls of Rome on the first stage of her journey to Hamburg. At two in the morning she was ready to start, and the procession began.

Driving across the Campagna that morning, meeting the stream of gay peasant carts on their way to Rome as the cool dawn crystallized into the magic of an Italian spring day, Christina wept. All day she was in tears, and that night she did not sleep, because to leave Rome was an agony scarcely to be borne.

" I would rather live in Rome and eat bread and water and have only a maid to look after me than possess all the realms and treasure of the world," she wrote later to Azzolino.

Yet the restless spirit of adventure drove her from happiness to the unfriendly North—to Hamburg where she was not needed, and to Sweden where she was not wanted. Her suite consisted of sixteen people, of whom the chief was the Marquis del Monte. Joseph Malaspina, Marquis d'Olivola, was also in attendance. He had been page to Christina since childhood and was half English, his mother being a Dudley of the family of the Earl of Northumberland. A contemporary describes him as " young and well made, extraordinarily handsome, and had a Bon Grace in everything he did. But he was a universal lover, and managed an amour like a Roman hero."

The Abbé Santini travelled as a secretary, Macchiati as her doctor, and Pezza as treasurer. Besides these went Clairet Poisonnet, Francesca Passaglia and Françoise Landini, the latter a *femme de chambre* whom Christina had picked up in Paris. She was a handsome girl, and when Christina found to her disgust—for she hated the sight of pregnant women—that Françoise was in that condition, she married her to her lover Landini, one of the executioners of Monaldesco, but not until a few days before the baby arrived. Landini himself was left behind on this expedition, but in Hamburg del Monte, as brisk as ever among the ladies, consoled Françoise for the absence of her husband, meeting her secretly at the French periwig-maker's, La Fortune, and the result of this intrigue, a pretty little girl, was adopted by Christina and baptized Marie. The child developed a fine voice and was with the Queen until her death.

However deep Christina's regret for Rome may have been, once the city was left behind there was no dallying on the road. With relays of horses they travelled night and day through Spoleta, Macerata, Ferrara, Legnano, Verona and Trent, and across the Tyrol, arriving on the 10th of June at Augsburg. Two carriages and a *calèche* were all the equipage for the whole suite, so that many had to go on horseback. Only one member of her company actually collapsed on the journey, and that was Malaspina. He was bad enough to need Macchiati's attentions, so they both stayed behind, while the rest, in varying stages of exhaustion, went forward, with Christina herself, as usual, lively and alert so long as excitement lasted.

After the Alps the pace slackened, though discomforts increased, with straw beds for the suite at several stopping-places, and poor food, for, once Germany was reached, the only consolation for absence from Rome was in sight. At Erfurt Clairet Poisonnet was sent speeding ahead to Hamburg. He was to travel day and night without a moment's delay. At Luneburg Christina was met by Texiera and Stropp, who brought the news that the Swedish Diet had been postponed indefinitely: they had other important things to talk about; but Christina was pre-occupied and would not listen.

Where was Poisonnet? He was to have brought her letters from Rome. That was why he had hurried ahead, so that she should have Azzolino's first letter addressed to Hamburg twenty-four hours earlier. But here was no Poisonnet, and everything was suspended until he could be found. For once he had overstepped the mark in his zeal for Christina. Knowing how passionately she desired the packet from Rome, he had gone beyond Luneburg to meet her on the road and had missed his way. At one o'clock in the morning he was found, and Christina spent the rest of the night scolding him and reading her letter. She had written thirteen times to Azzolino on the month's journey. Next day, the 22nd of June, she was in Hamburg, and at once established herself in a large house opposite the church of St. Michael, realizing that her journey to Sweden would be postponed. She had written from Rome to Bååt and Adami with instructions to announce her approaching visit. As she had never heard directly from the Regency as to the result of their Secret Commission, she asked for the free exercise of her religion for herself and her suite while in Sweden, and gave them an opportunity for revising their severe restrictions. Bååt's reply to her letter was waiting for her at Hamburg. It was not encouraging, and this decided her to buy the house in Hamburg and await Swedish developments while she and Texiera wrestled with her accounts.

There was a weekly post to Rome, and Christina never missed it. Her brilliant and self-revealing letters to Azzolino, all preserved by him, are the letters of a woman deeply in love. The imperious creature abases herself at the feet of the idol, and suffers the usual torments of the too ardent lover. The slightest coolness in his weekly letter sends her into an ecstasy of apprehension, and, though Azzolino's share in this long correspondence was destroyed by his own hand, there is no doubt from Christina's reproaches that many a cold blast served only to fan the flame of her infatuation.

In her first letter from Hamburg she sends him a million blessings for the affection he shows in his code letter; " the many tender sentiments it contains console me for all my sorrows ". His affection is returned by " the tenderest passion and the most ' L ' in the world ".

" I do not know if I shall ever be happier, but I do know that I ' R ' you till death."

They wrote in a secret code known only to themselves.

" Tell our poet," she writes later, meaning Azzolino himself, " his last verses are so beautiful that I admire them more than anything Petrarch ever wrote. . . . Everything you send me of his is divine, but this last ' *Hore un temps si breve* ' surpasses anything I have ever seen. If he goes on, he will become as famous on Parnassus as he is in the world. Please, have them put to music to be sung by Ciccolino, because I can tell from here how admirable the effect would be." Ciccolino was a favourite singer of Christina's who travelled with her to Germany.

A month after she arrived in Hamburg she writes that

she is distracted because she has no letter from Azzolino. She admits that to console herself she read the correspondence of Françoise Landini to get news of him. At least she knows that he is not ill. But what can be the reason of his silence? Her mind whirls with a hundred thousand fancies. But whatever the cause of it, she is sure it cannot be that he has forgotten her, or could ever lose an opportunity of writing to her. Her anxiety is beyond anything imaginable, and her only consolation for it is that her state of mind proves her feelings to be worthy of him.

When she has finished this agitated letter, two packets arrive from Azzolino, and one is the missing one. All is well then, and she is paid with interest for her anxiety.

She detests Hamburg and the Germans. She is well but extremely bored, and nothing can console her for absence from Rome. "Comfort me with your thoughts, and believe in the faithful and inviolable love I shall feel for you till death." "In most places it takes only twenty-four hours to make a day and a night; here an hour lasts twenty-four days, and those same days, which in Rome only endure a moment, last for centuries; and, if you have heard that I pace my room all night alone, you have heard the truth; and you might also have heard that I spend the nights weeping for my misfortunes, but this is a secret between you and me."

The chill was already noticeable in Azzolino's letters, and she assures him that whatever changes take place in his heart, nothing will change hers and she will be faithful to him till death.

"As for me, I am in a state which it would be painful for me to describe to you, and you must not be surprised if I do not reply to your *chiffres*, because I think my silence will speak better for me, and worry you less." In November she says: " All your coldness will not prevent me from adoring you *jusqu'à la V.*"

Christina's presence in Rome had begun to be irksome to Azzolino, in spite of a devotion to her which was genuine and deep enough. He had urged more strongly than anyone the importance of her journey North, and she could not help being bitterly conscious of his urgency. This doubt once planted in her mind would have grown to vast dimensions while she was away from him, feverishly preoccupied as she was all through her long absence from him. The constant reiteration of her faith in him only proved the doubt that was gnawing at her soul. She was wrong to doubt him for a moment. Whatever his *chiffres* may have contained of discouragement, his loyalty to her was always beyond question. Only he was, after all, a cardinal, with great prospects before him, and as the leader of the *escadron volant*, a marked man in Vatican politics. He was not yet, as Christina says, *papable*, but he would be one day; and meanwhile perhaps he was a little tired of scandal and pasquinades of which M. de Coulange's

Mais Azolin dans Rome
Sçait charmer ses ennuis;
Elle eût sans ce grand homme
Passé de trists nuits,

was only a mild example. His attempts to cool the correspondence were not successful; only a bitterness is added to the warmth. She is glad he had an amusing time at Frascati, and is grateful that he thought of her, but she is sure that when she returns to Italy (if she ever does return) she will find everything changed except her own heart. The threat not to come back, to settle in Sweden even, is constantly made at this time, to draw Azzolino, probably, but the effect is apparently negative.

He either does not believe in it or would not be too dismayed if it were carried out.

"Everything is frozen in this country except my heart, which is more ardent than ever," she writes on January 12, 1667.

Poor Christina! To her next letter she adds a postscript: "If Hamburg is not far enough away from Rome to satisfy your cruelty, I will go to the other end of the world and never return."

Worse was still to come. His next letter made very clear what earlier he had only hinted. She replies:

". . . I hope never to offend God, by His grace, and never to give you reason to offend Him either; but this resolution does not prevent me from loving you till death, and, since your vocation exempts you from being my lover, I exempt you from being my servant, for I wish to live and die your slave."

Azzolino was evidently attempting to modify their relations before Christina returned to Rome. Whatever those relations were, they had begun to be embarrassing, and with the probability of a conclave in the near future, and the absorbing occupation this would involve for him, he foresaw that the unrestrained adoration of the Queen would not help his work or his prestige. A slightly different footing—that was what he wanted.

Christina, in her hysterical state of mind, probably read more into his *chiffres* than he intended, and more and more she taunts him with such remarks as that she will be away at least two years. ". . . My return to Rome is not so near at hand as you fear. You shall not be bored by my presence for long, and if I can, as I hope, overcome Rome's fatal attraction for me, I shall go and seek a corner of the world where poverty is not a crime as it is in Rome." This last jibe was inspired by Azzolino's complaint of her extravagance and the impossibility of satisfying her creditors in Rome if she did not occasionally send him some money.

While shattering, emotional storms were crashing around her, she was working energetically at her money affairs. She would be sitting till dawn at her bureau, writing and calculating desperately. As the hated winter set in she scarcely went out; working, sleeping, eating, giving audiences and hearing Mass in one room. Her mild diversions were picquet and chess with del Monte and Malaspina, but not for money, she says, as she had none, and did not care to win from them. " Sometimes we talk of Rome and you, and dream of our return."

Her health was wretched. A persistent and " strange " pain in her side disturbed such sleep as she allowed herself. She never could sleep at all the night after the post from Rome arrived. Appalling colds which " furiously bothered her " with sore throats and endless headaches made the winter a burden. Macchiati told her that the colds were encouraged by her habit of sitting over the fire reading, but his diagnosis of her state in a private letter to Azzolino was, rightly, that it was emotional. He was anxious enough about her to call in the famous Jewish doctor, de Castro, but the result of their consultation was negative. She drank a great deal of milk, but it came from a tainted source, judging from her description of the dairy methods of Hamburg, and may have been responsible for some of her trouble. She refused to be bled, though she accepted the excellent suggestion of de Castro that she should play battledore and shuttlecock. Malaspina was her favourite playmate at this game.

Meanwhile, the winter dragged along, with few diversions. Clairet was nearly killed in a duel with one of the Italian servants. Del Monte and Pezza had leapt from their beds, hurried to the spot and tried to stop it when the news was brought to them, but they were too late and Clairet lay apparently mortally wounded. But he recovered, and Christina, in a postscript to Azzolino says, simply but with affection: "That beast Clairet is out of danger."

The news of Santinelli's marriage to the Duchess of Ceri came in March, 1666. The Duchess had been released from Castello Sant' Angelo in 1659, only to be incarcerated again by her mother, the Princess Cariati, for six years in Naples, when at last with Santinelli's help she escaped. They both wrote to Christina after their marriage, and she bitterly admires their effrontery for doing so. Santinelli's faithfulness to his Duchess through all those years may not have been entirely disinterested, but he appears to have settled down respectably in Venice with her. He had had the satisfaction of being ennobled by the Emperor of Austria, and his wife signs herself "Maria Aldobrandini, Marchesa di San Sabastiano". So his Viennese visit was not entirely fruitless.

The dreariness of Hamburg was relieved for one night, *Mardi gras*, by a gorgeous fête, which Christina explained to Azzolino she was obliged to give to amuse the ladies of the neighbourhood who were continually coming to pay their respects. But it was principally an opportunity for the Marquis del Monte to see how much he could make the Queen spend in one evening. He and Pezza worked night and day to convert a neighbouring tennis-court into an amphitheatre, and here a grand banquet lasting four hours opened the entertainment. The gentlemen drew lots for their partners, and thus the question of precedence in a mixed company of aristocrats and bourgeoisie was cleverly overcome. Macchiati was sent to Wismar to summon the great old General Wrangel, who was the most sympathetic member of the Regency as far as Christina was concerned, and was engaged in what was to him the negligible task of subduing the Duchy of Bremen. In spite of an attack of erysipelas, he consented to play the part of Godefroy de Bouillon in the ballet of "*Le Palais Enchanté d'Armide*". Christina led a procession of magnificent slaves, herself without jewels but hung with heavy gold chains—a symbol perhaps which Azzolino would appreciate.

Then there was a lottery for some handsome mirrors which Christina had bought for four thousand crowns, and on the sale of which del Monte was said to have made a decent profit. She won them herself, but gave them to Countess Wrangel. A ball followed, in which the Queen danced with great spirit. Those who watched her declared that she was like a goddess descended from heaven, says Santini. Christina was herself again that night.

The day after the fête she was so exhausted that she consented to be bled, and Macchiati had the satisfaction of relieving her of half a litre of blood which he says improved her appetite. The fête was the culmination of this visit to Hamburg, also nearly the limit of Azzolino's patience. She wrote him with a certain nonchalance that she had had a fête which she did not mention to him before in case it was not a success, but (now that it is over and it is useless to remonstrate) she assures him that she had revealed the gallantry and magnificence of Italy and France to a nation and town that had never imagined such a thing existed, and she herself was amazed at the good behaviour of the barbarous Hamburghers.

The Swedish Diet had been postponed so often that Christina despaired of ever reaching Stockholm if she waited for it. The Regency dreaded of all things her presence in the country and most of all at the Diet. "The idea of my presence in a Diet is to them the horror of horrors."

After several postponements the journey to Sweden was finally undertaken on April 28, 1667. The personnel of her suite had been approved by the Regency, Santini being described as "Secretary", though everyone knew he was a priest. The rest of her suite went with her, except Malaspina, who did not choose to be considered fit for the cold, wet climate of Sweden, and went to Spa to take the waters instead, returning thence straight to Italy. Malaspina had cleverly avoided the worst of the Rome-Hamburg journey by falling ill by the way and not joining the rest of the company with Macchiati until the Hamburg palace was quite comfortable. There was some trouble when he did arrive after having kept Macchiati on the road for more than a month while Christina's health was precarious and needed Macchiati her personal physician, but he was forgiven much because he had great charm.

For some reason the Swedish Regency had not been told that the journey had been postponed from the 23rd of February, which was the original and apparently the final date of her departure. Fortunately for her Italian suite, the hard frost had made it impossible for them to do the journey they were all dreading. In Stockholm, therefore, preparations were made as though she were setting out in February. The outward form was, as usual, carefully observed. An escort was sent out from Stockholm to meet her at Helsingborg. Count Pontus de la Gardie, younger brother of Magnus, and the Baron Per Sparre set off on February 23 with a company of equerries, gentlemen of the chamber, halberdiers and *palefreniers*, with carriages and horses from the royal stables.

Count Pontus was a fine young cavalry officer of heroic proportions, Count Sparre a handsome diplomat and man of letters. It was not till they arrived at Helsingborg that they knew of the postponement of Christina's journey. For two months they had to kick their elegant heels in a deadly provincial town, where a letter from Christina blaming the post's delays was but poor consolation for the lack of almost every comfort and pleasure that made life endurable, in a winter which even for Sweden was abnormally severe.

While they waited Christina began the journey to Sweden in a small open *calèche* which had been given to her by Wrangel. Though it was May the season was bitterly cold and wet, and Macchiati begged her to be prudent. Even her stoic obstinacy could not long withstand the piercing winds, and she took refuge in her coach. But not before she had contracted chill and fever, and become so ill, at Corsor, that she thought she was dying. Terlon, who was now ambassador at Copenhagen, came to meet her there, and brought the news of the Pope's death, which later turned out to be premature. But the shock of it reduced her to a state of fever and melancholy, and such restlessness that she would not stay in Corsor, but pushed on to Soro, a primitive place where she lodged in a damp, cave-like room and lay on an improvised bed, completely exhausted with fever and cold. Terlon had brought his French chef with him, and it was his excellent bouillon, "*brodi molto galanti, all'uso di Francia*", wrote Macchiati to Azzolino, that restored her strength. But she did not escape blood-letting, as Terlon sent to Copenhagen for his surgeon, who bled her in the foot. She writes to Azzolino that she was *deux doigts* from death. But the day after the blood-letting she was up and lunching with Terlon and attending to her affairs as though nothing had happened. The "poor Italians", however, were in a desperate state, all suffering from various forms of cold, cursing the unnatural climate and longing for home.

On the 16th of May she crossed to Helsingborg in a gay little gold boat of the King of Denmark's, which was quite unseaworthy; but the day was calm, and in less than an hour she was hearing the salvos of greeting from the Swedish men-of-war. An impressive company was waiting for her at Helsingborg, including, of course, Pontus de la Gardie and Per Sparre. Seven hundred cavaliers ("*gioventù veramente bella e bene a cavallo*", says Macchiati) presented arms as she went to the house that had been prepared for her. Del Monte was favourably impressed by the good taste of this house, which he conceded was worthy of Rome. He was especially pleased with the cloth of gold canopy and the gorgeous state bed in green velvet and gold.

In spite of the Regency's prohibition Christina did not forgo her daily Mass. Santini celebrated it the morning after they arrived in a private room to which no one but her suite was admitted.

The next day she set out in state on her way to Stockholm. Everywhere she was greeted with joyful enthusiasm. To the people she was still their Queen, loved daughter of Gustavus Adolphus the Great—and what should they think but that she had come to reign over them again? Here she was with her brilliant blue eyes and her radiant personality, illumining the dark landscape of oppressed Sweden, cheering the sad prospect with authentic royalty. For whatever their grievances may have been when she reigned, her people had suffered more since she had left them, and now that the hated Regency was in power, and there was no one but a puny child who was hardly a Vasa for them to acclaim, it was not surprising that the sight of Christina set the whole countryside through which she passed on fire.

No doubt the smoke of this conflagration reached Stockholm. Besides, news of a galley on its way to Stockholm, full of furniture for the Queen's use, had startled the Regency. It looked as though she meant to stay, and this must be prevented. For six days she made her triumphant progress among her people, and every day Santini celebrated Mass privately.

Then the Regency struck out. On the road Pontus de la Gardie had a letter from Stockholm in which he was ordered to tell Christina that the presence of Santini could not for another moment be tolerated in Sweden. This was obviously only a pretext. It was well known that Santini was a priest, and there could never have been any doubt that Christina would practise her religion in private wherever she was. Mass was celebrated each time behind closed doors with no one admitted except her suite, so that if the Regency had liked they could have overlooked it. But they did not like. They would have kept Christina out of Sweden if they had dared, but they knew that such a step would be their own undoing. The last of the true Vasas had by now become an ideal to the Swedish people. The reign of Charles Gustavus had been a sad one for them, and the prospect of being governed by de la Gardie for several years was not alluring. No wonder the wild acclamations which greeted Christina reached Stockholm and alarmed the already apprehensive Regency. Again they struck her in the vulnerable spot, and again the stroke went home.

She was for turning back at once in the first white heat of rage, but thought better of it and wrote an angry letter to the King, giving him an opportunity of changing his mind in this affair and reminding him who he was and who she was, and assuring him that he was not born to give orders to such as her.

While waiting for the final word from Stockholm she went on to her own town of Norrköping and did a certain amount of business there with Adami. She was no doubt soothed by her reception, which was clamorous, and decided to give a great banquet to her suite. While preparations were being made for it the reply came from the Regency to Pontus de la Gardie. Not only did they require the dismissal of Santini, but they decreed that if she went to hear Mass at the house of M. Pomponne, now French Ambassador to Sweden, she should go ostensibly to pay an ordinary visit, and this grace would only be extended to her for a few weeks. This was, of course, as good as ordering her out of Sweden.

"What!" she cried. "I am to go and visit Pomponne! If he were to propose that to me I would have him beaten! Yes, and in the presence of his own King, too!"

The banquet was abandoned. The royal escort was summarily dismissed, and Christina gave orders for the hire of post horses to carry her and her suite to the frontier next day. Young de la Gardie, ever mindful of externals, insisted upon escorting her himself as far as Helsingborg. Before she set out she drank an ironic health to the King, the Queen-Mother and the Regency, and left Norrköping in as ill a humour as possible, fearing one moment to be delayed and at another hoping to be recalled—cursing the slowness of ostlers when the horses were changed, and finally being dissuaded with difficulty from embarking at Helsingborg at dead of night, because, de la Gardie pointed out, it would look too like running away.

On the 5th of June she left her native land, never to return. As usual, she was sustained by nervous energy throughout the whole of this trying episode. But young de la Gardie wrote to the King that in all his life he had never been so overworked. His eyes were blinded by the dust and he could hardly stand upright. By the time the suite arrived at Hamburg everyone except Christina was completely exhausted. Del Monte and Pezza were half dead, and the women in such a sorry plight that they were unable to appear for several days.

Christina's gesture—finer propaganda than any number of Masses, private or public—was applauded throughout the Catholic world. Terlon, in Copenhagen, gave a great banquet to the Faithful and celebrated her splendid resolution. Meanwhile, she applied herself once more to the solution of her financial problems, suffering, once the excitements of the journey were over, from an excess of bile which Macchiati tried in vain to alleviate by bleeding.

CHAPTER XV

FIREWORKS

On the night of July 25, 1667, Christina's palace at Hamburg was a blaze of illuminations. The centre-piece represented the Eucharist among clouds, adored by angels, and beneath it was an allegorical figure of the Church treading Heresy underfoot. The Rospigliosi arms crowned all.

Alexander VII was dead and Cardinal Giulio Rospigliosi had been elected Pope. Christina had every reason for jubilation, because there had been a very strong chance of Cardinal Farnese succeeding to the Papacy. This would have been a disaster for her, because Farnese as Governor of Rome had made no secret of his disapproval of the Northern Queen and the conduct of her household. He had had to deal severely with her servants on several occasions for public misdemeanours, and sometimes had them beaten through the street. Then there had been a little unpleasantness on the Lungara—nothing really important, from a political point of view, but not helpful to their relations. The Farnese family owned a pleasure garden next door to the Palazzo Riario in Rome. The Cardinal loved to take his leisure in this retreat, which was known as the Vigna Farnese. He was as passionately interested in his flowers as Christina was in hers, and, because the wells of the Vigna Farnese were not inexhaustible, he bribed the keepers of the fountain of Pope Paul V, which was supposed to be reserved for Christina's exclusive use, to divert some of the water into his own garden.

"Very well," said Christina to her gardeners when she discovered this. "Pull down the palisades that keep his terrace from falling into my garden, and let us see what happens."

The terrace duly fell into her garden, and there it had to remain, because under the circumstances the Cardinal could not with dignity have the mess cleared up and a new wall built. Christina was never very good at reprisals, which always seemed to recoil on herself.

Rospigliosi had been Alexander VII's Secretary of State, and was one of Christina's closest friends. He was a great gentleman, with a cultured taste in all the arts, and a character that made him justly beloved. Christina had every reason to rejoice. But, however natural her delight at the result of the Conclave, her manner of showing it was perversely extravagant.

Hamburg was an exclusively Protestant city where the practice of the Catholic Faith was strictly forbidden by law. Any public demonstration of joy would be out of place, and might be to the detriment of Holy Church. But, deaf to the urgent appeals of the authorities of Hamburg, who prophesied disaster, she persisted in planning a feast which was to last three days, and to be inaugurated by High Mass in one of the rooms of the Palace. Court mourning for the consort of John Casimir of Poland, who had died a few weeks before, was abandoned. The Marquis del Monte, who was always at hand to encourage the Queen in extravagances from which he never failed to make handsome commissions, was the organizer of this ill-conceived affair.

Mass was celebrated, and so that all the world should know it, guns were fired at the elevation. These guns were placed in the square in front of the Palace. A grand banquet followed Mass, and the Prince of Hesse Homburg, who had been one of Christina's strongest dissuaders, was present. An enormous crowd had been outside the Palace for some hours, attracted not only by the prospect of fireworks, but by the two fountains of wine which were playing abundantly in the square. As soon as it was dark the front of the Palace blazed with hundreds of flares. The great set piece revealed itself; the swirling arabesques of fire illumined the inscription:

CLEMENS IX PONT: MAX: VIVAT

The Eucharist! The adoring angels! The Papal Diadem and Keys!

The cannon roared. The people shouted for joy, because a shout of joy is the only possible response to fireworks, whether they are in honour of the Pope or the Devil. Christina and her guests appeared in the square and stood among the crowd watching the enchanting spectacle. Though the Azzolino arms did not appear in the illuminations, this display was a secret tribute to the beloved Cardinal, for had not His Holiness himself sent word to her that he had made Azzolino his Secretary of State?

This was a momentous evening, and in spite of the scaremongers it had been successful, she thought. Standing on the steps of her residence, she looked back at the solid mass of human faces illumined by the already dying glow, and was not disquieted by the glint of the thousands of eyes turned upon her, nor by the thunderous clamour which greeted her retirement into the Palace. Detestable Hamburghers! They did not deserve such a glorious spectacle.

But as soon as she was gone the lights began to sputter, the glory began to fade, and, worst of all, the fountains of wine ran dry. The spell was broken. The Papal emblems—the crude symbolism, now blackened with smoke and dripping with foul wax, matched the rapidly changing mood of the intoxicated people. They had been captivated by beauty at first—exhilarated by generous wine. Now the stink of grease filled their nostrils, the darkness that followed brilliance and the aftermath of wine turned the excited crowd into a vengeful, dangerous mob.

The Queen bade her guests good-bye and retired to bed. Her room was in the front of the Palace, and she had not been there long when a shower of stones crashed through her window. The noise outside was now terrifying. The mob was trying to break into the Palace, and was hurling itself against the doors, which were hastily secured as soon as the danger was realized. Fortunately Christina's principal guests had not gone far. The Prince of Hesse and his friends had gone to the cemetery of St. Michael's church to watch the dying fireworks and the crowd, and hastened to the Palace when they saw the changed mood of the people. Hesse went to the Municipality for help, and another guest, the Count of Leiningen, to the Commandant of the town to ask for military assistance. The Commandant replied that he had been advised not to interfere, and by the time Leiningen arrived at the Palace with this news the situation was desperate indeed. It was obvious that Christina and her household were in peril of their lives. The mob was ferociously determined to storm the Palace, and there was only one way of saving it and themselves.

Christina gave the order to fire. The cannon which had saluted the Pope boomed again, musketry crackled, a deadly fire swept the square, and of the Hamburghers some fell dead and many were wounded. At this juncture the Commandant of the town, having changed his mind about coming to the aid of the Papist Queen, arrived with his soldiery and drove off the rest of the now terrified crowd, which was already flying from the scene.

By back streets, and carefully guarded, the Queen was escorted to the house of the Swedish Minister, where she took refuge for the night. But next morning she was round at the Palace, which was continually surrounded by a large crowd of curious people, among whom she walked unconcerned, giving orders for the necessary repairs, and in three days she was installed again as though nothing had happened. By way of reprisal she gave orders to her governors in Sweden to confiscate all Hamburg ships found in the ports of her island of Öland. As Hamburg had no trade with Öland, this act of hostility meant nothing at all, but the Regency, to make it clear to her that she had no power in Sweden, and further to humiliate her, forbade Bååt to take any notice of this command. Christina dealt generously with the families of the dead and wounded, and Hamburg seems to have resigned itself to her continued presence, for she remained another year engaged in the bitter task of dealing with financial problems.

Her leisure was spent in the laboratory of the famous physician and alchemist, Borri. She sought, as usual, the philosopher's stone. Borri was sufficiently notorious to have been burnt in effigy in the Campo de' Fiori at Rome after he had fled from a process for heresy. Over the Alps he fled to Germany and Holland, and wherever he went he performed sensational cures and miracles of alchemy. In Hamburg he did not find the philosopher's stone nor the solvent alkahest which, when found, would be, so it was said, even more potent than the stone. But he cured the Marquis del Monte of a serious malady, and, if a letter had not arrived from Azzolino telling Christina that Borri was an *excommuniqué* and that his presence in her Court was

TOMB OF QUEEN CHRISTINA, IN ST. PETER'S, ROME

not well seen at the Vatican, he might well have become a permanent institution. He was immediately dismissed, and went to Denmark, where he flourished under the patronage of Frederick III. Years later he died in captivity.

The excellent Adami was still in Sweden endeavouring to secure, once for all, the Queen's revenues. As well attempt to turn base metal into gold! After two years of disheartening effort he was succeeding with the renting of her islands, in spite of the Regency's delicately placed obstacles and the governor Bååt's open hostility. Bååt and Appelmann, who should have served Christina's interests, were creatures of Magnus de la Gardie, and there was no possible chance of easing her financial situation as long as the Chancellor was in power. He would see to that. Adami, though Christina had warned him, never quite gauged the perfidy of the Chancellor. The honest Italian was really working very hard, and did not deserve the constant criticism and haughty tone of Christina's letters to him. He had jealous enemies at Court, among them del Monte and Santini, and they were always ready to meet her moods of exasperation with a note of distrust.

Adami was at last so discouraged by her letters that he asked for his recall. Christina had no sooner given it than she began to dream of returning to Sweden. So Adami must remain. She wrote a polite letter explaining why his recall should be cancelled, but unfortunately the letter before that had openly accused him of dishonesty, a monstrous charge in the face of his loyal disinterested service. He left Stockholm at once, announcing there that the Queen had given him his *congé*, and arrived in Hamburg at the beginning of the year 1668. Christina was now conscious that she was losing a faithful servant, and attempted to be friendly with him.

"When I am on my way back to Rome, I hope I may see you at Loreto?" she said when he came to take his *congé*.

She always stopped at the shrine of Our Lady of Loreto (which was near Fermo, the birthplace of Azzolino and Adami) where she had left her diamond crown and sceptre, on her first journey through Italy.

Adami, proud and deeply wounded, merely said coldly: "If I happen to be at Fermo," and went from her presence without compliments. Before he left Hamburg for Italy he told del Monte and Santini and even, it was said, Texiera, what he thought of them. He had lost in the game of courtiers because he was an honest and simple soul. He lacked the graces of Santinelli, and he was not physically attractive to the Queen, which was the principal cause of his undoing.

Christina's renewed desire for Sweden was roused by the news that the postponed Diet would really sit in 1668. The usual wearisome exchange of proposals and negatives heaped up a mass of futile correspondence. While the Regency was quite firmly determined that Christina should never enter Sweden again, she on her side was only half-hearted in her attempt to do so. She knew her threats disquieted the Regency, and it was the only revenge she could take for the discomforts with which they encumbered her path. While she was always longing for Rome and detesting more and more the cold North, she was still a victim of ambition.

When someone remarked that she should console her cousin John Casimir of Poland for the loss of his consort, she said darkly: "I may sit on the throne, but not beside him."

John Casimir had reigned at Warsaw since 1648. He was a feeble degenerate and childless member of the Vasa family, and had been a cardinal before he came to the throne. When his wife died he chose to abdicate and return to the Church. Promises from Louis XIV of substantial benefices if he abdicated before September 20, 1668, hastened his retirement, and on the 16th of that month he formally resigned the crown.

Another empty throne!

There were four candidates for it; the Duke of Neubourg, the Prince of Condé, Prince Charles of Lorraine and the son of the Czar of Russia. There was not much to choose between them. The Poles themselves hated the French, Germans and Russians with good reason, but they favoured Condé because he was supported by the great Sobieski.

Christina determined to be the fifth candidate. Tradition was in her favour, and this was not the first time she had looked towards Poland as a possible solution of her ambiguous situation. Her sex was against her, but, as Azzolino wrote to the nuncio at Warsaw, Monsignore Marescotti, " all the world now looks upon the Queen not only as a man, but as superior to all men ".

The Pope approved of the project, though he had already promised his protection to the Duke of Neubourg and the Prince of Lorraine, but that was before Christina announced her resolve. So long as a Catholic ruled in Poland—that was the main thing. He issued a secret brief to the Polish Diet urging the election of Christina, " that heroine remarkable for her piety, her wisdom and her virile courage ".

Most enthusiastic of all was Azzolino. Whatever his motive for wishing to see Christina on the Polish throne, he worked without ceasing for that end. She was, he declared to Marescotti, born to command an army, to endure the privations of war. In support of this statement he instanced her long hours in the saddle without food or drink. (Many years ago this. Christina was now forty-two, and her health was uncertain.) Her courage and martial spirit only needed proving, said Azzolino. He did not stop at the praises of Christina. The abdicating King should be flattered; he might be useful. Hearing that he wanted to live in the Papal States, Azzolino offered him his own estate at Fermo. John Casimir found the idea attractive, and negotiations were almost completed when his stipulation that he should be allowed *liberté des femmes* brought the affair to an abrupt close. Azzolino was not going to have any ecclesiastical scandals in his own country if he could help it. John Casimir ended his days in France.

When the question of marriage came up, Azzolino hastened to assure Marescotti that Christina would marry whom the Polish Diet wished. Christina herself, when approached on this subject, merely agreed that she would not marry anyone to whom the Polish Diet objected. Then came the delicate question of the succession, and it was hinted that the Queen's age was against her providing an heir. At this Azzolino threw reserve to the winds. He declared (in confidence) there was no reason why she should not have a son, because her temperament was still so vigorous that there was every prospect of this possibility for another ten years. Whereas, in her youth, her excessive ardour might have prevented conception. This was from one man of the world to another. As the whole business was a profound secret, such clear evidence of Azzolino's familiarity with Christina's temperament need not go farther than the nuncio. This somewhat bewildered person was doing his best to steer between the various candidates so as not to lose the cardinal's hat which at least two of them were holding out to him. The Pope's strict injunction to secrecy made it possible for him when approached by Christina's emissary, Hacki, to put his finger to his lips intimating that by order of His Holiness the subject must not be discussed; so negotiations went slowly. Christina had also held out a cardinal's hat, but Marescotti had little faith in it, at first. As the months went by, however, and the massive correspondence of Azzolino and Cardinal Rospigliosi (nephew of the Pope) piled up the evidence of His Holiness's desire that Christina might be chosen as his candidate, Marescotti thought it prudent to divulge the secret of the Papal choice to one of the most influential electors, the Bishop of Posnanie.

When Marescotti whispered the name of Christina, the Bishop crossed himself several times and begged his friend not to joke with him. It was later made quite clear that the idea of a woman, however good a man she might be, would not be entertained for a moment by the electors. Azzolino and Rospigliosi were begged to save the Pope from disappointment and cancel the candidature of Christina, because there was no possibility of her being chosen. Fortunately the secret had been well kept and the cancellation could be done without much embarrassment to the Pope or to Christina. When the election took place there was no mention of her, and indeed the other four candidates had no better fortune than she had, for the Poles elected one of their own princes, Michel Korybut Wiesnowiecki, who burst into tears when he knew he was elected, reigned ingloriously for four years, and was succeeded by John Sobieski himself.

During the nine months of the Polish negotiations Christina was at Hamburg, sad and ill, hardly sharing the enthusiasm of Azzolino for the new project. Even the summer was cold and dreary. Fires were necessary in August, and she had constant headaches and sore throats.

Azzolino's letters were evidently full of reproaches, and he complained that he could not keep up her household without funds, and hinted that rumours of her extravagance in Hamburg had reached him. This subject always reduced her to a state of despair. His treatment will kill her, and, indeed, she longs to die. If he has so poor an opinion of her, why does he think her worthy to rule over Poland? And then, his cruel treatment will never change the unalterable affection that she will have for him —till death. That is always the sum of it. She will never cease to love him.

A few weeks before Christina left Hamburg for Rome, a very curious Englishman appeared on the scene. He was a Carmelite priest; his name was, according to Christina, " Cornicz ". He was on his way to Rome from England, which he had left rather suddenly. Christina, hearing that he was ill and a priest, sent such help as was necessary to him, and when he came to pay his respects she was, she declared to Azzolino, amazed at his appearance. He was clothed in a flame-coloured suit covered with ribbons, his hair was elaborately curled and he wore a *point de Paris* cravat " handsomer than my own ". This bright creature attached himself to her household, and was known as *il frate delle fettucie* because of the ribbons with which he decked himself. He spent his time drinking and meddling scandalously with Court affairs, and announced to the world that he was one of the Queen's gentlemen, whereas she says that she only spoke to him twice—once at the first audience, when she told him to change his habit, and the second time when she advised him to stop gossiping. It was not until she had to dismiss him for *choses indecentes* that she mentioned him to Azzolino, and then probably only because he would certainly go gossiping to Rome. He was such a type as

Christina might have been amused to study for a while, but a type that is inconvenient in a household.

It is not surprising that Adami should have revenged himself against his enemies as soon as he arrived in Rome. He visited Azzolino and revealed to him the perfidy of del Monte in particular, assuring the Cardinal that he and Santini were always ready to sell the Queen's secrets to the highest bidder, that del Monte was, in fact, a blackguard and a traitor and not fit to be in her service.

The result of this was that del Monte was sent to Rome by Christina, to justify himself or to die. Naturally he justified himself, and no doubt Azzolino was easily persuaded of his innocence. Another execution by Christina should at all costs be avoided. The Marquis returned triumphant to escort Christina from Hamburg, but he was a little late and met her on the road.

" I leave this place with the joy of a soul escaping from Purgatory—and I hope I have done a good part of mine here," she writes to Azzolino on the 20th of October. This is her last letter to Azzolino from Hamburg, written on the day of her departure for Rome. Its optimistic tone is not justified by events. She declares that she issues gloriously from the Purgatory that was Hamburg, and implies that the Swedish affairs are settled to her and, she is sure, to his, ultimate satisfaction.

On the contrary, those two years of struggle, sickness and unhappiness were years utterly wasted. She had better have been in Rome, among her books and pictures and her flowers, breathing the gold, sunlit air she so much needed, enjoying those precious days which " only endured a moment ". Whatever good came out of those two years had been accomplished by Adami in Sweden, for in spite of de la Gardie, his efforts had produced a slight improvement in the delivery, if not in the extent, of her revenue.

That was all. Sweden was definitely forbidden her during the King's minority, and the Polish affair was still undecided when she left Hamburg. Her genius, so prodigal and so perverse, had spent itself in perplexing calculations and gargantuan correspondence which led to nothing—nothing—nothing at all.

. . . .

Near Luneburg, on the way South, a cannon, saluting her, burst into a thousand pieces.

CHAPTER XVI

THE CONCLAVE

There was ample consolation for the barren Hamburg years awaiting Christina in Rome. At Narni Azzolino met her, and she had evidently taken more trouble about her appearance than on her last entry into the city. She wore an *innocente*, a long, excessively feminine garment, of purple velvet embroidered with gold, a yellow wig, a huge black feather in her hat, and a cape trimmed with *point de Venice*. The Pope's state coach with an escort of Swiss and other Guards conveyed her to the Quirinal, where she was received by His Holiness in an hour's audience. And again she was accorded that signal honour which marked her first arrival in Rome thirteen years ago. She dined with the Pope. That no woman was ever permitted to eat in the presence of His Holiness, whether she were empress, queen or relation of the Sovereign Pontiff, was one of the rules most strictly observed by the Vatican.

One does not hear of a sermon being preached at this repast as at the other. It was the meeting of old friends, and there were so many matters which both had at heart that conversation must have flowed easily. That Ottoman problem which was always at the back of Christina's mind —here at last was a Pope who was passionately interested in it. A union of Christian Europe against the Turk! Had not Christina aimed at that when she sent Gualdo forth on his fruitless eighteen months' tour seven years ago?

And now it seemed that Clement IX was actually accomplishing it, inspiring harmony in the jangling nations under his authority. Morosini of Venice, who had for two years been valiantly defending the last outpost of Christianity, Candia, against the invader, was being supported now by the Duke of Beaufort from France, by Vivonne and his galleys, by the ships of the Holy See and the Knights of Malta under the Pope's brother, Vincenzo Rospigliosi, and by an army of seven thousand men of France. This was the news which Clement had for Christina as they dined together that November day.

A grant of twelve thousand crowns a year from the Pope was only one among many blessings that came to Christina in the waning of 1669. Palazzo Riario greeted her as one is greeted by a home that has shared vividly in great happiness. As she entered the Palace her countenance was alight; she looked " plump, pink and white, and enchanted with her return ". Perhaps those dead years in Hamburg were worth while after all, to contrast with the glowing autumnal garden which had so fantastically grown up in these two years. The Vigna Farnese terrace no longer intruded, and the lemon trees still carried their shapely fruit.

Best of all her blessings was the honour done to the beloved Azzolino. He was the most powerful man in Rome—the trusted servant of His Holiness. He had arrived; one day, she dreamed, he would be Pope, but not too soon.

Meanwhile, life was splendid in the Golden Age of Rome. Noble diversions filled the days and nights. The ugly shadow of nepotism which had hung so blackly over the pontificate of Alexander VII was gone. There were certain offices which went by tradition to the Pope's relations, but there was no enriching of the Rospigliosi family at the expense of the Holy See. Clement IX combined the best kind of worldliness with a generous integrity probably unique in his day. The social life of Rome had never been more brilliant. One day there was the magnificent entry of an ambassador, another a pageant or the promotion of a cardinal, among the public festivals, while the private entertainments were on a scale never surpassed. Every night there was the opera, at which Christina was constantly seen in her gorgeous box. She was responsible for the introduction of female sopranos, who enchanted Rome with their singing and beautiful clothes. In her box a constant visitor was Cardinal Odescalchi, who, when he came into power some years later, changed his ideas and dealt severely with the theatre, and female singers were heard no more at the opera.

Every evening the bells of Rome rang, reminding the faithful to pray for the gallant defenders of Candia. The Pope himself never ceased to pray for the cause which meant, literally, life itself to him.

Alas, for the human element which defies Divine interference! The foolish Duke of Beaufort had no sooner arrived on the scene than he rushed his troops into action, in spite of the entreaties of Morosini, with disastrous results. A concerted attack a month later ended in tragedy, and two hundred heads of French leaders, including Beaufort's, were paraded before the Grand Vizier. The French, discouraged, and impatient of the prudent Venetians, deserted their allies and set sail for home. Vincenzo Rospigliosi, helpless without the French, was also obliged to retire. The news was slow in reaching Rome. It was six weeks before, on October 13, Clement IX heard of the tragedy. The deep anxiety he had been suffering all through the summer was now made manifest. At the shock of the news he collapsed, and less than a fortnight later he was seized by apoplexy.

He lingered through November, and well aware that his end was approaching, he held a convocation in his room, with thirty-six cardinals round his bed, gave the purple to half a dozen prelates, and finally spoke a Latin discourse in which he begged them to elect his successor without discord or self-interest, to the glory of God. He deplored his own failure, and it was clear that his mind was unceasingly occupied with the tragedy of Candia. He sent for Christina a few days before he died and bade her a tender farewell. She left his presence in tears, and indeed the death of this good man was a most bitter blow for the Church, and for Christina and Azzolino a misfortune incalculable.

No time was wasted by the factions at the Vatican as soon as the illness of the Pope was known to be fatal. The most active of all was Azzolino. His manœuvres at the last Conclave had been astonishingly successful. He had managed so skilfully that both the French and Spanish parties had given him the credit of having worked for the election of Rospigliosi in their favour. Both factions were, for once, entirely satisfied, and the *escadron* had issued from the Conclave with its colours flying.

The coming Conclave was of enormous importance to Azzolino. He had immediately selected Cardinal Vidoni as the desirable successor to Clement IX. Vidoni came from a noble but not princely house in Cremona, and had been nuncio to John Casimir in Poland. He was acknowledged to be just and honourable and a man learned in affairs. There were those who feared his justice might degenerate into severity, the last quality to be tolerated in a Pope, but there was a strong general feeling in his favour.

As soon as the funeral ceremonies of Clement IX were over, the Vatican was invaded by Bernini's workmen, who transformed the whole of the first floor into a network of little cells in which the cardinals should be immured until the Pope be elected. The distribution of cells, like the entire business of the Conclave, was supposed to be under Divine guidance, but we find Azzolino conveniently placed in cell 18, which looked out on the Borgo Nuovo, where Christina was eagerly working for him in Palazzo d'Inghilterra, which she had taken in order to be within the precincts of the Vatican and so free to exchange notes without interference. In cell 19 was Ottoboni, Azzolino's principal friend and one of the live wires of the *escadron*, and in No. 20, singularly enough, was Vidoni himself. Cardinal Flavio Chigi was also indulged, for he was in No. 59, which not only faced south-west, but looked out on the piazza of St. Peter's where he could watch his horses at their daily exercise. He had been made cardinal when he was twenty-one by his uncle, Alexander VII, and was remarkable for his equipages, his kennels, and his peculiar tastes.

Chigi was now thirty-four, and leader of a powerful faction which included Vidoni, Azzolino's choice for the Papacy. Christina said of this faction that it contained twenty-two men and twenty-five Popes. Of the twenty-five members of it, all coveted the tiara, but three of them were not, she considered, men. These three were Flavio, his cousin Sigismondo, and a Tuscan cardinal, Nini.

The two Crown factions were led by d'Este, Barberini and de Retz for France, and by de Medicis for the Spaniards. Then there was the Rospigliosi faction, and finally the *escadron volant*, also called the Pamphili, of which Azzolino was the acknowledged leader. Pamphili was no longer cardinal, being married to the famous and beautiful Princess Rossano, but he and his wife were active in the work of the *escadron*. Much too active, Christina thought. This princess had known Azzolino before he met Christina, and rumour said it was not only poetry that he had dedicated to her in the past. However this might be, an annoying incident occurred when Clement IX lay dying. Some of the *escadron* cardinals paid a call on Vidoni, who was spending a little leisure at Frascati, and afterwards took him to visit the Princess Rossano. When he was presented to her, someone said:

"This is the future Pope."

When Christina heard of this she was justly annoyed. The first principle of making a Pope was that no one should know whom anyone else was backing. That someone should have announced Vidoni as the coming Pope before the *escadron* had begun its stealthy campaign on his behalf, was exasperating. It did not, however, prevent Christina from throwing herself with more than her usual zest into the novel excitement of a conclave. Because Azzolino had, temporarily, it was to be hoped, lost his official quarters in the Vatican, she took the house on the Borgo Nuovo for him for three years. It eventually became his permanent residence until he died. Here she set up her work-room, from which she was in constant communication with Azzolino, sometimes writing as many as four long notes a day, and sometimes, when there was a lull in the correspondence, walking in the little garden of the new house, whence she could see the barred window of cell No. 18, where the beloved was weaving his invisible threads so cautiously—so dexterously, she fondly thought.

She had been among the friends who visited the cells on the last day before the Conclave, on the 20th of December when the gates were to clang on the outer world until the Pope was chosen. An excellent law of the Middle Ages to guard against abuses was no longer in force. By this the members of the Conclave, strictly secluded as now, were given their food through a carefully guarded window, and, if the Pope were not elected in three days, only one course was allowed. After five days bread and water was the only fare, with a little wine. Things were not so severe now, but they were bad enough. Clement IX had chosen an unseasonable time to die. The Vatican was never comfortable in winter, and the cells, inadequately warmed with unwholesome braziers, were not at all to the taste of the cardinals, accustomed as most of them were to luxurious living. Food, too, if it was not actually handed through a window, was, however richly and pompously presented, generally half cold. One cardinal quite definitely refused to occupy his cell, and that was Ludovisi, a member of the *escadron*, to whom laziness was a point of honour. This was so well known that his cell, No. 60, had not even been furnished.

Under the somewhat meagre circumstances it was natural that a half-bottle of wine or a few dozen oysters might well turn the scale in a delicate manœuvre. An excellent claret played a lively part in the Conclave. Cardinal Medici writes to the head of his family:

> Bouillon and Retz tell me that they have gained new life from Your Highness's claret. Please send me some more. I will distribute it by the bottle, for unless I give it to them decanted the conclavists will take to tippling.

Vidoni was one of the first to be tempted with oysters and claret. He was genuinely shocked by this, especially as it was Lent, and immediately went to Azzolino for advice. This was, that to keep on good terms with the tempter, it would be best to accept a half-bottle of claret a day. "With these people, it's the only thing to do," he said.

One does not hear what Vidoni did about it, but he

is scandalized by the eating and drinking that goes on. " Think what the Protestants will say," he writes.

When Christina said good-bye to Azzolino on that last day she also visited the cell, next door, of Vidoni, and inaugurated her career of duplicity with the remark, made in ringing tones to be heard by as many as possible:

" Here at any rate is one who will not be Pope! "

A trifle overdone this. Crude and Nordic. Later on, when she had had more experience of Latin diplomacy, she took to heart Azzolino's advice, which was to tell the truth in order not to be believed. " It is," he wrote to her, " the art of arts."

The problem of electing a new Pope was a hard one. To begin with, no one must have any ambition to be Pope. Everyone *papable* must, naturally, wait for Divine guidance to direct the Conclave. There were no candidates; there were " subjects ". Then each faction must scrupulously conceal from the others the secret of its choice, but as soon as the Pope was elected it was absolutely essential to have been responsible for that election.

Azzolino, though he was next door to Vidoni, never entered his cell, and was never seen speaking to him. They exchanged notes at night, and Azzolino took the trouble to translate Christina's long notes from French into Italian for the benefit of his subject. Christina, on her side, when she was not in her work-room in Borgo Nuovo, was giving audiences to the French and Spanish Ambassadors, the Duc de Chaulnes and the Marquis d'Astorga, and most of the notable people interested in the Conclave. The Riario became the centre of intrigue, and her business was, with as much mystery as possible, to convince all her visitors, whatever faction they favoured, that Azzolino was Pope-maker, and to him alone would be the credit, whoever was elected. The atmosphere inside and outside the Vatican was indeed so heavily charged with intrigue and mystery that it looked as though the cardinals would be immured for ever. The weeks went by, and one by one the subjects were juggled with and excluded by vote. If Vidoni were elected there was no doubt that Azzolino would be re-established and more powerful than ever, therefore Chigi, who had favoured Vidoni until he suspected that Azzolino did too, looked round for another subject for his party. Already D'Elci, the most *papable* of his own faction, had been excluded, and he at last confided in his own people that he would seek a subject elsewhere. When Azzolino heard this he decided upon a daring ruse which was, in fact, scarcely worthy of his intelligence nor a good example of the "art of arts".

He wrote a note to Christina saying that, for all he had apparently been working in favour of Vidoni, the very opposite was the case. Vidoni, he wrote, was the strongest of Chigi's candidates, and for that reason most to be feared. As to whom the *escadron* was truly favouring—ah! that would be known all in good time. Meanwhile, Christina would please go on giving the impression that Vidoni was his favourite, which was the best way of getting him excluded.

This note, written on the 25th of February, he carefully dropped so that a servant of Chigi should pick it up, and it was, as he had hoped, taken straight to the Cardinal. But Chigi was not at all taken in by it, and the only result of the trick was to prejudice him still more against Vidoni. There was another unfortunate incident of the same kind. When D'Elci and Bonvisi had been excluded after an enormous amount of intrigue and disappointment, there was a strong move in favour of

Odescalchi, so strong that by the 16th of March there was little doubt that he would be elected; so little that the luxurious Ludovisi actually visited his cell, in spite of the cold, which was regarded as a sure sign that the end was near.

Now Odescalchi was one of the *papables* whom Azzolino had completely neglected throughout the Conclave. Not a word or sign to him of favour or friendship. This must be remedied at once. An inspiration came indirectly from Cardinal de Retz, who was said to have congratulated Odescalchi upon his approaching election. A note should be written to Odescalchi in the same tone, and what could be more effective than the statement that he, Azzolino, had advised de Retz to pay that little compliment, thereby convincing Odescalchi that the leader of the *escadron* had been working secretly for him all the time, and that his apparent indifference was but a mask to hide the truth?

An excellent idea, but unfortunately, as this was the first note Azzolino had written to Odescalchi, the servant of that cardinal, suspecting a mistake, as of course it had no direction on the outside, handed it to the servant of Cardinal Bouillon in the cell next door, with whom Azzolino was in constant communication. Bouillon read it and passed it on to de Retz, and the result was not pleasant for Azzolino. Apart from the de Retz invention, which was trivial and foolish, the impression made on these two friends of his was that he had been working against them secretly in favour of Odescalchi. Azzolino was decidedly losing ground in Vatican politics. And in the end Odescalchi had only seven votes in the scrutiny of March 20.

The discomfort of the Bernini cells and the intense cold soon began to tell upon the immured cardinals. Fever and bronchitis laid many of them low, and even

Azzolino, one of the youngest and strongest, was shut in his cell for several days with a violent cold. When he was better he sent a note to Christina telling her so, and her joy at hearing it was surpassed by the fact that he had written the two letters " S.M." at the head of it. S.M. —Sua Maesta? It meant more than that, and no one but themselves will ever know what it did mean, but on Christina those two initials had a magical effect:

> But under what happy influence did you give me that glorious reminder of my past felicity? Am I mistaken, and do the letters " S.M." no longer mean what they used to mean? If I could describe to you the joy the sight of them gave me, you would think me somehow worthy of that title, which is dearer to me than Queen of the Universe. But I cannot be worthy of it, since you have deprived me of it. Do what you please; I am yours so absolutely that you cannot without injustice and horrible cruelty doubt that I deserve " S.M ".

In his answer he gave her " S.M." again, but for the rest of the Conclave he was discreet, and begged her to be the same. Business and sentiment were so carelessly interwoven that it became impossible to show her letters to his friends. He asks her to separate from " other things " the affairs of the Conclave.

These affairs went on all through Lent. Easter came, and Christina retired for a week to the Carmelite convent in Lungara as was her habit. This time she said she would not have objected to a slightly deaf confessor. The cardinals, still imprisoned, were engaged solely in their religious observances. But soon they were busy again, with their secret votes and daily scrutinies, and now it was spring in Rome, and the cells were warmer, and everyone hoped the end would soon come.

It came in the last days of April, and a shattering end it was for Azzolino. It was incredible! De Retz had been plotting with Chigi and Rospigliosi to such purpose that the future Pope was already decided upon without the slightest reference to Azzolino. A very old gentleman, Cardinal Altieri, had been chosen. His principal recommendation was that he was eighty years of age. The news was brought to him in his cell, and he broke down and begged with tears to be allowed to die in peace, crying that he was too old and not capable of what would be expected of him. He clung to the bed he was sitting on when the conclavists came to carry out the custom of pillaging his cell. He was then seized and led kindly but forcibly to the Sistine Chapel, where the vote was made. Still the old man protested, and only after an hour's persuasion would he consent to wear the Papal insignia.

The election was announced to the waiting crowd, the smoke from the voting papers rose to the skies, the barriers that had shut out the world for over four months fell, and the first to kiss the Pope's toe was Christina herself. Her bearing, of course, was brave, but her heart was sore for the man she loved.

Reams of paper and gallons of ink! The usual reckless expenditure of energy and enthusiasm, and, as always, disillusion at the end.

"*Mon Dieu*," she had written to Azzolino when the cabals were at their thickest, "*si vous pouviez profiter de tout ce desordre pour vous même!*"

But he had failed. Flavio Chigi had beaten him in the "art of arts".

CHAPTER XVII

AND LAST

The ancient Altieri took the title of Clement X, and surprised his electors by lasting for six years. He had little influence, as was expected, upon the life of Rome, which went on as gaily as in the reign of Rospigliosi. Christina rose from the ashes of her Conclave failure and became a brilliant centre of intellectual life.

From Vatican politics to the Arts. The savants flocked again and the spate of panegyrics was prodigious. It was useless for Christina to try and stem it. "No panegyrics!" was her order to the academy which gathered weekly in the shady garden of the Riario. But the poets ventured to disobey. Her own copy of Pignatelli's book dedicated to her is in the British Museum. She has read it carefully and made excitable marginal notes. "This is not at all to the point. Only laughable," she says when she is compared to Alexander the Great. "*Non è vero!*" "*Non sta bene!*" "*Non lo posso soffrire!*" occur frequently. But when Pignatelli says: "Born Woman, Your Majesty has become Man: nay, more than Man!" she cries in the margin: "*Quest' è bello, bellissimo!*"

Sitting in her box at the opera, with her cardinals around her, she could not look away from the stage without encountering the malicious eyes of the Grand Constable's lady, Maria Colonna, who, a few years ago had supplanted her sister Olympe Mancini in the affections of Louis XIV.

Now Maria Mancini was the first and much the most amusing hostess in Rome. Throughout the Conclave she had been a continual provocation to Christina. Her parties at Palazzo Colonna were spectacular, and no one could resist them. All the beautiful women in Rome could be met there, whereas at the Riario one encountered nothing but men, and if one were not careful one was caught in a recitation of supreme dullness and length. True, there was always delightful music at the Riario, and brilliant conversation, but the atmosphere was sometimes oppressive, with Christina too much preoccupied with playing her part for the good of the Church to be quite her high-spirited self.

The Palazzo Colonna was especially gay while the Conclave was going on, because Maria's naughty sister Hortense had fled from her tiresome old husband, Meilleraye, disguised as a boy, and had arrived in Rome with nothing but a maid. Her beauty was amazing, and it was not surprising that the Duc de Chaulnes, the Marquis d'Astorga, and their gentlemen should prefer dancing at the Palazzo Colonna to talking politics at the Riario. Maria Colonna had actually suggested that Christina should shelter her sister when she discovered, even before the Conclave, that she had been too indiscreet. That was a pretty idea, indeed, when it was all Christina could do to endure the sight of her own respectably married ladies-in-waiting in that condition. And as though Hortense needed sheltering!

There were ways and ways of leading ambassadors into the right political path, and the Mancini way was not and could not be Christina's. There was no doubt that Palazzo Colonna was a stronghold of the Chigi faction, and when it was known that Hortense had been dressing up as a slave, in the slightest of garments, luring de

Chaulnes into a private cabinet—even though her sister was present and the interview lasted but a quarter of an hour, and the French Ambassador had come from it with the air of one who *n'avait pas donné contentement*—Christina wrote indignantly to Azzolino of the danger of these hussies, a letter which the Cardinal called an " elixir vitæ " and read to all his friends of the *escadron*, omitting, it was believed, one or two sentences.

It had been a tug of war all those four months between Christina and the two scandalous sisters, and the sisters had had the best of it. No wonder that their continual presence in the box opposite Christina's was intolerable. She complained to the Grand Constable himself, and he said that if he moved his box he would also move the whole theatre. She turned to the Pope, and he was scarcely more helpful. He pointed out that since she had to tolerate the presence of a large crowd of common people in the theatre, she could hardly object to the presence of one of the first families in Rome. In the end she was pacified by an order that did not remove the Mancinis, but decreed that all gentlemen present should be uncovered while the Queen was present. A good deal of talk was caused by the sight of a large notice attached to Christina's box which ran:

Indulgentia plenaria pro Purpuratis.

The significance of this was that, Christina's box being always so crowded with cardinals that they were unable to sit down, they were to be exempt from the general rule. But it was an elegant inspiration for the pasquinades which were so popular at the Palazzo Colonna.

When Clement X died, Christina was fifty, but Azzolino's surmise when he was working for her election to the throne of Poland was correct. She showed no sign of age, and her health was better than ever before. Bourdelot was giving her good advice from Paris, but, when he told her not to eat so much, she was justly indignant. " A man may be as temperate as he likes—he can't eat less than I do. You say I have done well to give up wine, which I have not given up, because I never drank it." Christina's taste was still simple, and she enjoyed eating chestnuts with her maids a great deal more than sitting down to a solemn meal. To Bourdelot she also wrote her indignation at the publication of Chanut's alleged Memoirs, which contained pages of disgraceful slander about herself. It was proved later that, as she thought, not Chanut her good friend, but the venomous French Minister who followed him, Picques, had added the slanders to Chanut's own work.

She was never to leave Rome again. There were to be no more agitating journeys and heartbreaking absences. Azzolino, less occupied than she could wish at the Vatican, was yet on that account more than ever at the Riario, and their friendship grew and flourished with never a withering leaf. She worked, but only a little, for the Conclave of 1676. She was interested in Cardinal Conti, because he was a relation of the Duke of Poli, one of her gentlemen. But it was a half-hearted business, because it was a foregone conclusion that Odescalchi really would be Pope this time. As Innocent XI he ruled severely, being especially hard on those diversions which he had enjoyed in his cardinal days. Experience had cured Christina of reverence for the wearer of the fisherman's ring. " I have known," she wrote, " four Popes, not one of whom had common sense." When the edict went forth that *décolletée* for ladies was to be strictly forbidden—it was said that the Pope's spies confiscated too deeply-cut garments—she arrived with her ladies for an audience clothed in angelic white garments, *innocenti* run riot, and convulsed the Court with mirth. Public festivities were forbidden at carnival time, therefore Christina organized an enormous fête at the Riario. So it went on—she defied the Pope on every possible occasion.

The scandal of freedom of Quarters was a very real one, and the Pope attempted with a bold hand to sweep away the privilege of ambassadors of immunity from Roman law. This immunity had been abused by foreigners who took up residence in the neighbourhood of their ambassadors, so that the greater part of Rome became sanctuary for all sorts of criminals, male and female. All the embassies submitted to the Pope's new decree except France, and Christina, who had been given the same privilege as the embassies, was, surprisingly, one of the first to accept it. But on the first possible occasion she defied it. A seller of contraband spirits, caught by the Papal police on Easter Day, hiding in a church, escaped from his captors, and tried to find refuge in one of Christina's coaches, which was standing near by. It was locked, so he clung on to the padlock with such strength that it was impossible to drag him away. The police were obliged to get him off by putting a rope round his neck and nearly strangling him. Such an act of violence and disrespect to the royal carriage brought an excited and indignant crowd to the spot. The Queen herself came out from Mass, and when she heard what had happened sent Landini with one of her valets and commanded the police to release the prisoner, " or she would know what to do ". Such a vague threat alarmed them, and they delivered him up without more ado. The result of this affair was that Landini and the valet were condemned to death by the Pope. Christina declared that if they died they should not die alone. It was a long business, but nobody died, and in the end the Pope merely said in explanation of Christina's conduct, "*È donna*", which annoyed her more than anything that had gone before.

In Sweden the young King had shown his mettle, and before he came of age he appointed a commission to inquire into the doings of the Regency, which was found guilty of extravagance and had to pay an enormous sum to the Crown. As soon as Magnus de la Gardie fell, the affairs of Christina began to brighten, and though her revenue was never delivered in full, what there was of it began to come in regularly. She never ceased to agitate about it, and financial security was never to be hers. But whatever she had had, it would not have been enough, and she lived and died in a state of splendid insolvency.

One of the greatest moments of those twenty years in Rome came when she heard the news of Sobieski's victory over the Turks at Vienna in 1683. She wrote to him: ". . . Your deed shows you to be worthy not only of the crown of Poland, but of the monarchy of the whole world. . . . I feel envious, a sentiment which until now was a stranger to me. I do not envy you your kingdom, nor your treasures and spoils, but your title of Liberator of Christianity."

She was now fat and round, looking smaller than ever, with a double chin, but a merry wit which never failed her. She confessed to Mlle de Scudéry that she dreaded old age, and would prefer death: and death came long before she showed any signs of age, though it spared her till she was sixty-three.

In 1672 she had sent the Marquis del Monte to Sweden to see to her affairs. Somehow he managed to return in a year with so large a sum of ready money that he was made Grand Master of the Horse, a post which had been vacant since the death of Monaldesco. Her insistence that

the hundreds who lived upon her bounty. But in less than three weeks she died, with Azzolino kneeling beside her in her gaily frescoed room at Riario. Before she died she sent to the Pope to ask his pardon for her behaviour, and he sent absolution by his nephew, Cardinal Ottoboni, and a message that he wished to come himself to give her his blessing. But he did not come, it was said because he was ill. As she felt her strength going she signed her will in which she left everything, except a few legacies, to Azzolino. She died magnificently, as bravely as she had lived, going forth as gallantly to meet the God she did not fear as she had years ago set out in her vain search for freedom.

She lay in state wearing the white dress she had designed, the royal crown on her head and the sceptre in her hand, surrounded by three hundred candles. In her will she expressly asks that she shall be buried simply, without any lying in state, and that there shall be no funeral pomp, her epitaph to be simply:

D.O.M.

VIXIT CHRISTINA ANNOS LXIII

neither more nor less. Her requests for no ceremony were never obeyed in her lifetime, probably because no one supposed that she meant it, and no doubt in the same spirit she was given a funeral of imposing magnificence and a tomb of prodigious size.

The Sibyl had seen clearly. Only two months after Christina's death came the end of Azzolino. The destruction of their correspondence which she had commanded was only half done. It is not surprising that he kept hers to the last. Few would have the will or the strength to destroy such pledges of rare affection as those letters of Christina to her Cardinal lover.

Not one of her great visions and schemes had materialized. Nothing flowered—nothing bore fruit. And now even the disposition of her estate went wildly astray. To Pompeo Azzolino, nephew of the Cardinal, fell the priceless treasures of the Riario. He was the last person on earth she would have chosen as her heir, an insignificant member of her household whom she had not even mentioned in her will. He did not get much out of it, however, for there were twenty thousand Masses for the repose of Christina's soul, as well as two chapels in St. Peter's, to be paid for out of the estate.

The library was bought by Cardinal Ottoboni, who later was Pope, and most of the furniture and pictures were acquired by various noblemen whose obligation to pay was lightly regarded. So lightly that Pompeo was moved to appeal to the Swedish King, who showed himself quite indifferent whether Christina's heir should get his legal rights or not. Christina was dead, and Sweden's obligations were ended.

BIBLIOGRAPHY

The following are the principal authorities consulted:

Mémoires pour servir à l'histoire de Christine, Reine de Suède. (4 vols.) ARCKENHOLTZ.
Christine de Suède et le Cardinal Azzolino, BARON DE BILDT.
Christine de Suède et le Conclave de Clément X, idem.
Mémoires de Madame de Motteville.
Mémoires de Mademoiselle de Montpensier.
Lettres de Gui Patin.
Indiscrétions de l'histoire, A. CABANÈS.
Ménagiana, MÉNAGE.
Bayle's Dictionary.
Siècle de Louis XIV, VOLTAIRE.
Historia della Regina di Svetia, GALLEAZZO GUALDO.
Vita di Alessandro VII, CARDINAL PALLAVICINO.
La Regina di Svezia in Italia, G. CLARETTA.
The Swedish Archives.
Journal of the Swedish Embassy, BULSTRODE WHITELOCK.
The Diary of John Evelyn, edited by AUSTIN DOBSON.
Christina of Sweden, F. W. BAIN.
Denmark and Sweden, JON STEFANSSON.
The History of the Intrigues and Gallantries of Christina, Queen of Sweden, translated from the French.

This last book has been cautiously used, and the attractive *Lettres Sécrètes* resisted altogether, because the best authority considers them forgeries.

Beyond the books I have mentioned, I have had the benefit

of my husband's incomparably versatile library, where I found many surprising treasures.

I am greatly indebted to the late Baron de Bildt for his advice; to M. Henry Bordeaux of the Académie Française for sending me the text of his discourse, made at Stockholm in May, 1927, on the subject of Christina; to Mrs. Douglas Goldring for her patience in reading through the typescript; and most of all to M. Louis Zettersten, of Stockholm, who made my task lighter by his practical interest and kindly encouragement.

INDEX